University of Cambridge Department of Applied Economics

OCCASIONAL PAPER 51

DISAPPOINTING MARRIAGE: A STUDY OF THE GAINS

FROM MERGER

DAE OCCASIONAL PAPERS

Other titles in this series may be obtained from:
The Publications Secretary,
Department of Applied Economics,
Sidgwick Avenue,
Cambridge, CB3 9DE

Disappointing Marriage:
A Study of the Gains
from Merger

G. MEEKS

'In marriage, a man becomes slack and selfish, and undergoes a fatty
degeneration of his moral being.'
Robert Louis Stevenson

CAMBRIDGE UNIVERSITY PRESS

CAMBRIDGE

LONDON · NEW YORK · MELBOURNE

Published by the Syndics of the Cambridge University Press
The Pitt Building, Trumpington Street, Cambridge CB2 1RP
Bentley House, 200 Euston Road, London NW1 2DB
32 East 57th Street, New York, NY 10022, USA
296 Beaconsfield Parade, Middle Park, Melbourne 3206, Australia

© Cambridge University Press 1977

First published 1977

Printed in Great Britain at the University Printing House, Cambridge.

Library of Congress Cataloguing in Publication Data

Meeks, Geoffrey.
Disappointing marriage.

(Occasional papers – University of Cambridge, Department of Applied Economics; 51)
Bibliography: p.
1. Consolidation and mergers of corporations – Great Britain. I. Title. II. Series: Cambridge.
University. Dept. of Applied Economics. Occasional papers; 51.
HD2741.M43   338.8′3′0941   77-3896

ISBN 0 521 21691 5 hard covers
ISBN 0 521 29234 4 paperback

Contents

List of tables

List of figures

Acknowledgements

I am very grateful to a number of institutions and to many individuals for help in preparing this study.

Much of the work reported here was supported by the Esmée Fairbairn Charitable Trust, which financed a research project at Edinburgh University, headed by Professor G. Whittington, to develop and exploit a data bank of quoted companies' financial accounts. The study has then been further developed for publication during my tenure of a Social Science Research Council Postdoctoral Fellowship at Cambridge University. At this latter stage the Cambridge Department of Applied Economics and especially the Cambridge Growth Project have provided valuable research facilities.

Officials of the Department of Industry, particularly Mrs W. R. Borland and Mr P. G. Reeve, were a willing and efficient source of help and advice at many stages during our preparation of the data bank. Mrs A. G. Harris, Mr L. Morris and Mr W. Watson gave valuable support in programming the computer. Mrs D. C. Hathorn repeatedly met unreasonable deadlines when typing various drafts of the work. Ms J. Bradley and Dr C. Day helped with editorial advice.

Last but not least, four people read earlier versions of the whole book and offered constructive criticism and advice, much of which was accepted. Professors P. Vandome and K. D. George, respectively supervisor and external examiner of my Edinburgh Ph.D. thesis, from part of which the book originates, suggested a number of improvements to the work. Professor G. Whittington first introduced me to company accounts as a fertile field for economic research, set up the project in which this book started, was an energetic Ph.D. supervisor, and has given help generously on all aspects of the work, not least in the sparsely populated frontier region between economics and accounting. Finally, Dr J. G. Meeks, my wife, subjected the text to a philosopher's scrutiny, spotting and helping remedy arguments that were incomplete, suggesting fresh ones and greatly improving the expression: remaining shortcomings on these scores are more likely to reflect my stubbornness than her lack of assiduity. From this it will be clear that the book's title contains no element of autobiography.

1

Introduction[1]

Should the state assume a restrictive or a permissive policy towards the merger of private sector companies? This issue is important both because of the conflicts between current policy prescriptions from economists and because of the scale which merger activity has sometimes reached. Prescriptions range from the outright ban[2] to almost unqualified approval.[3] Perhaps more surprisingly, the opponents of merger can span the political spectrum,[4] whilst some advocates of *laisser-faire* vehemently attack and others vigorously defend unbridled merger activity.[5] And the potential scale of merger activity in the United Kingdom (to be suggested more fully in chapter 2) can be illustrated by the fact that, in the period 1964 to 1971, the average continuing member of the quoted company population actually relied more heavily on growth by merger than on net new investment in fixed assets.[6] This book attempts to resolve the policy issue by presenting new evidence on recent British mergers.

The structure of the study

Some indicators of the past scale of merger activity having been presented in chapter 2, chapter 3 tackles the key issue of whether mergers have fostered efficiency. In the light of the generally unfavourable findings there, chapter 4 examines the role of the capital market in allocating the finance necessary to effect mergers. The subsequent chapter asks first whether growth by merger is the preserve of very big companies; and then attempts to answer the question: does growth by merger inhibit new investment? And the final chapter draws together those results of earlier chapters which bear on state policy towards merger.

In addition there are appendices, which have been used for two purposes. From

1 Despite differences in the strict legal meaning of some of the terms, a number of names are used for the merger process and its participants, most of them culled from the literature. All are used synonymously, but to give variety. The process is variously called (growth by) merger, takeover, acquisition and acquisition of new subsidiaries as well as external growth. The participants are called acquirer and acquired company, parent and new subsidiary, predator and victim. Although some of these terms might suggest that the acquired company is an unwilling party to the merger, this is of course not always the case: the victim's management is often enthusiastic for the takeover and may sometimes have initiated it.
2 See e.g. Rowley and Peacock (1975) who argue for a ban on a major class of mergers, and the discussion of these views in chapter 3 below.
3 See e.g. Hindley (1973), and chapter 3 below.
4 For instance, hostility towards merger is to be found both in Rowley and Peacock's (1975) assertion of free market principles and in Singh's (1971 and 1975) critiques of company sector *laisser-faire*. See chapter 3.
5 See chapter 3.
6 See below. This finding might surprise even those whose theories do take account of take-over as a means of expansion. For instance Penrose (1959) writes that 'only in depression could acquisition be the dominant form of expansion . . .'.

appendix B onwards they incorporate relatively tedious detailed material: wherever possible, supplementary results, detailed definitions and lengthy surveys of earlier work have been relegated from the main body of the book, so as to avoid cluttering the argument. Thus these three appendices are included principally for reference. However, the appendix to chapter 3 and appendix A have a rather different role. Their arguments augment those in the main text, but go into more detail than is necessary to sustain the central point.

The data

The basic data bank used in the study contains the standardised published accounts, supplemented with other financial information, for all but the smallest U.K. quoted companies for the whole period, 1948–71 (a fuller description of the bank is provided in appendix B) – providing information (e.g. on income, expenditure on additional assets, share and loan issues) central to the questions raised in this book. The total contents of the bank, then, amount to five or six million observations, some two million of which may be used in a single chapter. Thus, whereas earlier work on the topics studied here has often reported the experience of, say, no more than 50 companies,[7] a thousand or more contribute to the analysis here. And the strength of the conclusions which emerge derives to some extent from the fact that they are based on so great a mass of observations.

But quantity is not everything. Some might concede that the number of observations furnished by these accounting data was adequate, but question whether their quality passed muster. However, whilst admitting that the data are not perfect (what data are?), one might still retort that, at the very least, this information is extremely carefully prepared. A vast army of clerical workers is employed within companies to document individual transactions and to assemble these detailed records into the accounts; a smaller army of independent auditors is devoted to verifying the accounts and ensuring their conformity with standard practice; and the accounting institutes aim to secure consistency of treatment between companies by reviewing a large sample of published company accounts every year,[8] and, at least in recent years, by issuing statements of what standard accounting procedure is to be. As well as often being the best information on the firms' activities available to shareholders, creditors and sometimes managers too, the information resulting from all this activity serves as the ultimate source of data on which company tax assessments and much of national income accounting are based.[9]

Nevertheless, the information *is* imperfect. Inconsistencies of treatment do survive the controls just detailed, producing data for particular variables which are not strictly comparable between companies. Appendix B discusses difficulties which, though pervasive, are not expected to distort the results presented in this study in any systematic way. There are known to be particular accounting problems attending takeover, however: appendix A is devoted to a discussion of them, developing the method of removing potential bias which is used in chapter 3.[10]

7 See appendix C for a survey of some earlier work. One significant part of the study, in chapter 3, examines rather fewer than the thousand companies generally included: it examines some 450 selected participants in merger.
8 See Chartered Accountants' Trust for Education and Research (1972).
9 It seems anomalous that 'accounting data' should have become almost a pejorative term in economics, even though these data are the foundation of much national income accounting which still maintains its respectability among economists.
10 Sometimes there are known to be other accounting biases which cannot readily be quantified and taken into account directly; so in these cases the bias is noted and the conclusion made a qualified one.

2

The scale of merger activity in post-war Britain

This chapter documents the scale of U.K. merger activity in the post-war period, comparing its importance with that of other means of company expansion and providing some indicators of its contribution to companies' overall growth. Anyone who is already convinced of the quantitative importance of growth by merger is invited to bypass the detailed description which follows (perhaps reading the summary at the end of the chapter) and join the main argument in chapter 3.

Table 2.A provides an annual series for aggregate expenditure on new subsidiaries[1] by the 893 companies which continued in independent existence within the Department of Industry (D.I.) quoted company population for the period 1948–69.[2] In money terms the level of this expenditure has risen very steeply over the period; and the rise must have been pronounced in real terms too, since inflation alone would have produced only a doubling within this period.[3] Indeed, as the rest of Table 2.A shows, the *growth* of expenditure on takeovers has outpaced that on investment in fixed assets[4] (whether taken net or gross of replacement investment):[5] whereas in the early part of the period purchases of new subsidiaries represented

1 Trade investments (the acquisition of shares in companies connected through trade) were also included in this category of expenditure until the separate classification of trade investments was abandoned following the 1967 Companies Act.
2 1969 was chosen as the closing date because many companies were excluded from the D.I. population thereafter: in particular a new higher minimum size criterion was applied for the inclusion of a company in the population. This limits the number of companies surviving from 1948 until after 1969. Some (lesser) changes in the definition and hence membership of the D.I. population also took place prior to 1969 (see appendix B), so that only by focussing on the experience of a *continuing* set of member companies can changes in company behaviour be distinguished from mere changes in the membership of the population.
  Other sources generally neither do this, nor provide the averages given in Table 2.B, but can be useful in other respects. The chief large-scale studies for the United Kingdom (Singh (1971) and Kuehn (1975)) have concentrated on the victims' experience. Others (e.g. Aaronovitch and Sawyer (1975), Utton (1971)) have emphasised the contribution of merger to industrial concentration. Rose and Newbould (1967) provide some data on the takeover record of all D.I. quoted companies prior to 1967. And of course the prime source of aggregate data on takeover is the D.I.'s publication, Business Monitor (M7). Additional data based on this source for recent years are given below.
3 See Central Statistical Office (1972), Table 16. The upward trend is somewhat exaggerated, however, as the D.I. changed to a less conservative basis for valuing takeovers from 1964 (see appendix A).
4 In such comparisons 'investment in fixed assets' always excludes the purchases of the new subsidiary's fixed assets in the course of takeover.
5 Replacement investment is for this purpose assumed equal to depreciation, following conventional practice. See the discussion below on whether this convention is warranted.

Table 2.A   Aggregate expenditure on new subsidiaries and new investment in fixed assets, by the 893 companies which continued in independent existence within the D.I.quoted company population from 1949 to 1969

Year	I Expenditure on new subsidiaries	II Expenditure on gross new investment	III I as percentage of II	IV Expenditure on net new investment	V I as percentage of IV
	£ million	£ million		£ million	
1949	13	176	7	96	14
50	11	187	6	100	11
51	−25	213	−12	114	−22
52	11	222	5	115	10
53	36	238	15	116	31
54	72	304	24	162	44
55	60	382	16	216	28
56	76	509	15	316	24
57	86	529	16	312	28
58	83	502	17	254	33
59	201	464	43	188	107
60	202	570	35	262	77
61	243	725	34	380	64
62	344	707	49	327	105
63	251	746	34	317	79
64	341	869	39	379	90
65	328	1075	31	517	63
66	228	996	23	375	61
67	482	1061	45	380	127
68	1295	1244	104	441	294
69	628	1427	44	544	115
Averages:					
1949–55			9		17
1956–62			30		63
1963–69			46		118

Notes: Derived from own computations using Edinburgh Data Bank (no consistent series is available giving this information in published government statistics). The basis of valuation of expenditure on new subsidiaries changes to a less conservative method in 1964: see appendix A. Expenditure on gross investment includes investment financed with investment grants: companies often net these grants out of investment; but they are added back by the D.I. as part of their standardisation procedure. For fuller definitions see appendix B.

only a very minor percentage of gross investment, the later years saw this expenditure equal towards half of gross investment, and in one year (1968) actually exceed the whole of it.[6]

6   There are difficulties in obtaining data for subsequent years which are comparable with earlier periods (see above); but the best available indices – for this expenditure for all industrial and commercial companies – show the following picture (1964 = 100):

1964	'65	'66	'67	'68	'69	'70	'71	'72	'73	'74	'75
100	102	99	163	385	185	195	158	439	226	95	59

(derived from Department of Industry (1975), Table 8). A varied picture emerges for the years since the close of the period studied: on the one hand the figure for 1972 is unprecedentedly high, whilst, on the other, very recent years have witnessed much more modest activity. It seems unlikely, however, that this lower level of activity will be permanent: merger rates have tended to fluctuate considerably in the past and a revival of interest in merger already seems apparent (see Times (1976)).

Table 2.B   The contribution of takeover and new investment in fixed assets to the growth of the typical continuing company, 1948–64 and 1964–71

	1948–64		1964–71	
Rate of growth (% of opening net assets, per annum):				
by net new investment in fixed assets	3.7		4.4	
by acquisition of net current assets	2.4		1.4	
together = *by internal means*		6.1		5.8
by acquisition of subsidiaries:				
for cash and by share for share exchange	2.1		4.9	
by taking on minority interests and long term liabilities of subsidiaries	0.8		1.1	
together = *by external means*		2.9		6.0
of total net assets		9.0		11.8
Net new investment (as above)		3.7		4.4
'Replacement investment'(identified with depreciation)		3.8		5.5
Gross investment		7.5		9.9
Number of companies		1250		966

Notes:

All variables are simple averages across all company – years.

All variables are expressed as a percentage of opening net assets before averaging.

Table 2.A and most of the subsequent analyses exclude minority interests and long-term liabilities acquired with new subsidiaries from expenditure on takeovers.

The acquisition of subsidiaries is valued on a more conservative basis prior to 1964: see appendix A.

For fuller definitions see appendix B; for the full accounts of the 'typical' company, see appendix D.

One reservation attaches to the picture given here for the increase in these forms of expenditure; for of course the purchases of new fixed assets and of subsidiaries by victims which were acquired after the beginning of the period will be included in the (continuing) predator's expenditure in later years (i.e. after acquisition), but not in earlier ones. Thus rising expenditure by continuing companies could in principle be consistent with stable expenditure by companies in aggregate: the continuing companies could simply be extending their share of total activity. However, while this qualification does affect comparisons between years of the level of either form of expenditure, it is unlikely to alter the comparison between the two forms of growth: purchases of subsidiaries were increasing at a considerably faster rate than purchases of fixed assets.

This broad picture for the aggregates is complemented by the results in Table 2.B, which analyses the growth of the typical continuing quoted company into its various components, including growth by takeover. For two populations, those companies which continued in independent existence within the D.I. population from 1948 to 1964, and those which continued from 1964 to 1971,[7] these components of growth are expressed as a percentage of opening net assets for each company-year and the results are averaged across all company-years within each period. A comparison of the two periods shows that the typical overall growth rate of net assets in the later period was higher than that for the earlier years (11.8% p.a. as against 9.0% p.a.).[8] However, the rate of growth by means other than takeover (net investment in fixed assets, and in net current assets) was actually slightly lower in the second period.[9] The increase in the rate of net asset growth can be wholly attributed to the increased expenditure on new subsidiaries. Moreover, in the second period this external component of growth exceeded the internal components: taken alone, it actually contributed 6% p.a. to the growth rate of the typical company.[10]

However, the comparison is slightly less marked for gross investment in fixed assets: this includes that part of investment financed from depreciation provisions, and exceeds growth by acquisition in both periods. This additional component of investment is not of course included in the conventional net asset growth measures, since it is reckoned to correspond to the consumption of existing capital and hence not to augment the capital stock of the firm. But gross investment figures are included here because, as is argued in Meeks (1974), this supposed correspondence is in practice far from exact, and for some purposes there could be a case for concentrating on the firm's gross outlay on new investment.

Table 2.B relied on averages: Table 2.C considers the distribution of the values underlying them. It reports features of the distribution of companies by three growth measures, expansion by takeover, net new investment and gross new investment. Two characteristics of acquiring companies are prominent. Firstly, quite a large proportion of companies (of the order of a sixth) made no acquisitions at all during the sixteen- and seven-year periods considered, whereas relatively few companies committed no expenditure at all to investment. Secondly, for both periods, whilst the middling ranges (especially 5 to 10%) are more highly represented in the case of net investment, at the upper end of the distributions at least as many achieved extremely high rates of growth by acquisition as did by net investment.

Indeed, as calculations reported in appendix D show, in 1964–71 the top 100 in the ranking by growth by acquisition achieved an average rate of external growth of

7   1964 is chosen as the dividing point because it marks both a change in the D.I. population and an alteration in the basis for valuing takeovers (see appendix A).
8   This assumes that the change of population between the two periods does not distort the comparison. And there is the further qualification that the change in the basis for valuing takeovers in 1964 (see above) does exaggerate the increase both in the rate of growth of net assets and in the rate of growth by takeover.
9   See the discussion in Meeks (1974) of the arbitrariness of the distinction between net and replacement investment; and on the typical shortfall of replacement investment below depreciation.
10   What is more, the relatively great reliance on takeover by giant companies, documented in Meeks and Whittington (1975b), means that, as the aggregates suggest, averages of the growth variables weighted by size would reveal an even greater role for growth by takeover than appears in the unweighted averages given here.

Table 2.C Percentage frequency distributions of firms classified by different components of growth

Range (% p.a.)	Growth by:		
	Takeover	Net new investment	Gross new investment
1948–64			
0	16.2	7.4	0.9
<5	73.0	72.0	37.5
<10	6.7	17.1	42.3
<20	2.9	2.9	17.1
<30	0.7	0.4	1.6
<50	0.4	0.2	0.4
⩾50	0.1	0	0.2
Total	100	100	100
1964–71			
0	19.5	6.3	1.0
<5	56.3	63.4	22.1
<10	10.5	21.2	42.9
<20	8.4	7.5	26.0
<30	2.3	1.2	6.0
<50	2.0	0.4	1.9
⩾50	1.0	0	0.1
Total	100	100	100

Notes: There are 1250 companies included for 1948–64, for 1964–71 there are 966. The variables are defined in the same way as in Table 2.B., which gives the respective averages (see appendix B for detailed definitions).

28.6% p.a.,[11] markedly higher than the rate of growth by net investment (14.5% p.a.) and higher even than the rate by gross investment (26.0%) achieved by the top 100 according to that variable. And the companies which grew so rapidly by acquisition were able to combine this external expansion with above average growth by internal means, to achieve an overall rate of growth of net assets of 37.2% p.a. This means that the average member of the top 100 by acquisition was practically doubling its size every two years.[12] Moreover, this growth rate is an average sustained over seven years, a fact which prompts reservations over Newbould's (1970, p. 148) conclusion that the 'inability of firms to merge repeatedly is empirically confirmed'; and it is 10% p.a. faster than the average growth rate of the

11 It might be objected that the mean is not wholly appropriate as a measure of central tendency when the distribution of values is so skewed. It does, however, have advantages over, say, the median in yielding mutually consistent estimates of the typical contribution of individual components to the overall growth rate (as in Table 2.B).
12 Size is admittedly measured in money terms, but the inflation of around 6% p.a. which prevailed in this period would not seriously affect this result.

top 100 by gross investment (27.3%).[13, 14] This evidence then lends some support to Penrose's (1959, p. 210) proposition that 'the possibility of acquiring other firms raises enormously the maximum rate of expansion, primarily because it substantially reduces the managerial services required per unit of expansion'.[15]

Summary

Expenditure on new subsidiaries has been rising dramatically over the post-war period, until in the years 1964–71 it accounted for slightly over half of the net asset growth of the typical company, exceeding net investment in fixed assets. The contribution of merger to growth varied a good deal among companies however. At one end of the scale, a significant minority of companies committed no expenditure at all to acquisition during each period – a more unusual situation in the case of investment. At the other end of the scale, the fastest growing companies by acquisition have tended to reach rates of growth significantly higher than those achieved by the fastest growers by new investment.

13 The ranking is the same in the earlier period, but the differences are smaller – partly as a result of the valuation differences mentioned above and discussed in appendix A.
14 The difficulty of distinguishing between net and replacement investment (see above) must also be borne in mind in these comparisons. Replacement investment (by definition equal to depreciation) represented about 7% of net assets for these intensive acquirers in the second period, but 11.5% for the top 100 by new investment.
15 See below, especially chapter 5 and the appendix to chapter 3 for further discussion of Penrose's arguments.

3

The efficiency gains from merger

Theoretical presumptions

Advocates of *laissez-faire* face a dilemma over state policy on merger. On the one hand, the very idea of denying private companies the freedom to merge is anathema. Lord Robbins (1973) expresses this position:

'Speaking as one who is persuaded by the main principles of economic liberalism — to put it mildly — my feeling about policy relating to mergers and takeovers is that there is a certain presumption against preventing people from buying or selling such property as seems to them to be desirable.'

But on the other hand, as Rowley and Peacock (1975) emphasise, merger typically entails a further departure from those conditions of perfect competition in which the *laissez-faire* ideals would best be fulfilled. And whereas Lord Robbins lends his weight to those arguing for few if any restrictions upon merger, Rowley and Peacock support an outright ban on a major class of mergers in order to safeguard the conditions under which *laissez-faire* can operate effectively.[1]

Those favouring the freedom to merge might also appeal to the economic benefits to which such a policy should lead. Why would firms merge if it did not pay, they would ask: as Hindley (1973) argues, the sale of a business takes place only when 'the buyer . . . has higher expectations of its future profitability than the seller'. And if it is assumed that these higher expectations are fulfilled after sale and that higher private profitability is associated with social gains, such as lower resource costs per unit of output,[2] then the anti-interventionist case will indeed be strengthened. The assumptions of the case may be supported by arguments and evidence on the potential social gains which might be realised by merger. It could be argued, for instance, that where excess capacity exists in an industry, output might be concentrated in existing least-cost plants. Or the reduction in market uncertainty on the merger of two former rivals might act as a stimulus to investment in new lower cost equipment. Or again the concentration of output in the hands of a single producer might enable him to realise the potential economies of scale which, the evidence

1 Joan Robinson (1964) neatly expresses this dilemma (p. 136):
'Another question on which orthodoxy has led us into great confusion is monopoly. Generally, in the orthodox scheme, monopoly is a Bad Thing. Professor Knight has been known to attack the United States' anti-trust laws as an illegitimate interference with the freedom of the individual, but for most economists competition is absolutely essential to the justification of *laissez-faire*; it is competition which equates the margins, distributes resources so as to maximise *utility,* and generally makes the whole scheme work.'
2 The relationship between profitability and efficiency is discussed in detail below.

9

suggests,[3] are available in many British industries. Or, finally, takeover might lead to the better management of existing assets.

However, a number of rival arguments leave the efficiency conclusions in doubt. The first has already been suggested: many economists convinced of the general case for *laissez-faire* argue that merger weakens the competitive pressures within the economy, which, if fully effective, should preserve the efficiency both of individual units and of markets and ensure the harmony of private and social interests. And it has been economists of this persuasion, rather than advocates of government intervention in general, who have pressed the case for tight government curbs on merger. But if, further, it is admitted that conditions in economies such as the British diverge widely from those of perfect competition, then the scene is set for a number of alternative theories — not tied to the *laissez-faire* case — which offer no presumption that merger will enhance efficiency.

These theories presume that the divorce of ownership from control, documented as early as 1932 by Berle and Means, is well advanced — that many major companies are controlled by salaried managers with little or no ownership interest in the firm: were these managers free to choose their goals, there is no necessary presumption that they would engage single-mindedly in the pursuit of income for the owners. And these theories do indeed maintain that, in many sectors of the economy, the competitive pressures on the firm (in product and/or factor markets) are not sufficiently strong to constrain managers to maximise profits.

One strand of such theory stresses that rigorous cost minimisation and the relentless pursuit of profit are likely to be uncomfortable for managers. Leibenstein (1966) cites evidence for his contention that:

> '. . . firms and ecomomies do not operate on an outer-bound production possibility surface consistent with their resources. Rather they actually work on a production surface that is well within that outer bound. This means that for a variety of reasons people and organisations normally work neither as hard nor as effectively as they could. In situations where competitive pressure is light, many people will trade the disutility of greater effort, of search, and the control of other peoples' activities for the utility of feeling less pressure and of better interpersonal relations.'

On this account, a takeover which offered the *prospect* of higher profit, either through improved trading terms or lower average costs for the combine, might in the event prompt not an improvement in profitability but a relaxation of effort on the part of management, or, in Leibenstein's terms, an increase in 'X-inefficiency'.[4,5]

A closely related theory (Cyert and March (1963)) also abandons the assumption that managers either choose, or are compelled by market forces, to pursue profit

---

3 See Pratten and Dean with Silberston (1965) and Pratten (1971). Though the authors qualify any implication that merger should be vigorously pursued in order to achieve scale economies with misgivings about the concomitant decline in competitive pressures (see the discussion of competition below). Also, one of the authors has expressed considerable scepticism over the importance of scale economies as either a motive for or consequence of takeover (see George and Silberston (1975)).

4 As well as a possible longer-run effect of diminishing the pressure on management to reduce costs in order to steal a march on the rival or else in response to the rival's cost cutting initiative.

5 See Hicks (1935) for an early recognition that profit is likely to be sacrificed to the quiet life when competitive pressures are weakened.

single-mindedly. On their argument, imperfect markets create a permissive environment in which achievements can depend on aspirations, which themselves display considerable inertia. This 'behavioural' theory sees management's aspirations as relatively stable in the short term. If this is so, then a change in the firm's environment which has the *potential* of yielding higher revenue or reducing costs may not be accompanied by any significant improvement in profit: either the firm may fail to realise potential benefits at all or else it will absorb these benefits in less efficient production or administration. Thus Cyert and March 'predict that the costs of firms that are successful in the market place will, *ceteris paribus,* tend to rise'. Their example of a propitious development which might lead in this way to higher costs is a cyclical upturn; but the enhancement of market power or the potential reduction in unit costs brought about by a merger lend themselves to the same treatment. An easier life for the firm's employees (especially the managerial groups) and not an increase in profit is on their argument the likely result.[6]

A further strand of recent theory of the firm emphasises the sacrifice of profit maximisation not to the 'quiet life', but to the alternative maximand of growth. Several factors suggest that the pursuit of growth might loom large in managers' calculations: these are dealt with in detail by Marris (1963, chapter 2, and 1964). Not only does greater size typically bring the directors of a company greater power and prestige; but, other things equal, it also brings more stable performance[7] and greater immunity from takeover.[8] In addition it is typically accompanied by higher salaries for directors.[9] It is not immediately clear, however, that the objectives of profit and growth need be in conflict. Indeed, Marris discusses circumstances in which the two variables will be positively associated: only a low rate of profit may be available to the slow-growing, unambitious firm which relies heavily on 'old' products with low or declining profitability. A more active pursuit of new products and markets, accompanied by greater expenditure on research, development and marketing, might produce at one blow both more rapid growth and higher profitability.[10] For all that, however, beyond some point the relationship *is* expected to be inverse: one might adduce accelerating marketing or research costs necessary to

6   The authors give some (casual) evidence for their argument, and incidental support for their case appears in other contexts. For instance, Reddaway's (1970) investigation of the effects of SET revealed that 'where SET had been reported as having an effect on policy with regard to self-service or self-selection, it often emerged that this would have been profitable before SET, but that SET had provided the impetus to carry out the change. In other words, it was the 'shock' effect of SET rather than the change in relative prices of different inputs which was responsible . . .'.
        Thus, in Leibenstein's terms, the firms were working within their 'outer-bound production possibility surface'; and, following the Cyert and March argument, aspirations and performance lagged behind potential achievement.
7   See, e.g. Whittington (1971) and Meeks and Whittington (1975b).
8   See, e.g. Singh (1975) and Whittington (1972).
9   For U.K. evidence on this topic see Meeks and Whittington (1975a) and Cosh (1975). These papers also give an account of results for the United States. There is some evidence that pay depends on profitability too, however; so it is not clear that a growth policy which entailed a lower rate of profit would produce a net salary gain. This issue is dealt with in more detail below.
10   Not only is higher profitability likely to accompany more rapid growth for such reasons, but also greater profits will help finance growth. On this finance relationship see below, especially chapter 4.

sustain further improvement in the growth rate, or the famous 'Penrose Effects' — the problems of assimilating a very large number of new additions into the management team.[11] And these difficulties again give rise to some scepticism over the profitability consequences of growth by merger.

There is, then, no consensus among economic theorists on the effects of merger on productive efficiency. There is a sharp conflict of views among the defenders of *laissez-faire* on the gains or losses from merger in a competitive system, whilst arrayed against the sanguine advocates of free merger is a range of theories questioning whether efficiency gains are a motive for or consequence of merger.

However, to some observers the issue still might not seem so unresolved. They would argue that the chief fruits of merger were not to be found in its participants' subsequent performance but in its role as a control mechanism upon inefficient management. Hindley (1973, p. 23) provides a version of this case: 'So long as bidders threaten managements producing poor results, the economy would probably gain from the general spur to efficiency even though the taken-over assets themselves were operated with the most appalling incompetence': a discipline which recalls that attributed by Voltaire to the English navy: 'In this country, we find it pays to shoot an admiral from time to time to encourage the others'. Of course, the *laissez-faire* opponents of free merger discussed above would derive little comfort from this position, since, on their argument, this spur to efficiency was only being bought at the expense of the more conventional control mechanism of competition in product and factor markets — which merger typically weakens. But there are also empirical counters to this claim. Singh's (1975) study concludes that, judging by survival statistics and the incidence of takeover, the pressure upon managers to raise profitability in order to avoid takeover is weak, especially for larger companies,[12] and that: '. . . as a survival strategy, attempting to increase relative profitability may well be inferior to attempting to increase relative size, particularly for larger unprofitable firms' (p. 510). On this argument, growth by merger (which chapter 2 suggested was the path to really rapid growth) could be the very means for a company to avoid unwelcome takeover of itself — even if it yielded no efficiency gains to the combine. Paradoxically, then, the takeover mechanism might provide not a stimulus to raise efficiency[13] but an incentive to embark upon yet more takeovers. That the takeover mechanism has been relatively permissive towards unprofitable companies is further corroborated by Whittington's (1971) evidence that large numbers of companies with poor profitability records have survived for long periods without being taken over: 96 U.K. quoted companies achieved an average profit rate over the twelve years, 1948–60, of less than 5% p.a. compared with an average for the 1955 continuing members of the population of 16.6%.

Thus existing evidence does not suggest that takeover is a potent disciplinary

---

11 See Penrose (1959).

12 Whittington (1972) reports that 83% of the top 12 companies in 1948 survived until 1968 (a much higher proportion even than for other members of the 1948 top 100). And these very biggest companies control a quite disproportionate share of the national economy: in 1970, for instance, the top 12 companies accounted for some 25% of the net assets owned by the entire 1200 quoted companies in the D.I. population (source: own calculations).

13 A challenge to some of Singh's results on the disciplinary role of takeovers has appeared in Kuehn (1975); but a rebuttal is to be found in Singh (1976).

force, so that its merits on that score alone override the many other considerations outlined above: conflicting predictions of the efficiency consequences of merger based upon diverse theoretical presumptions still leave the issue of state control quite unresolved. Accordingly, this chapter attempts to resolve the issue by seeing which theoretical position has been supported by the *evidence* of past mergers.

The need for a presumption

Some might argue that the variety of theoretical views illustrated above is entirely appropriate, reflecting the diversity of possible circumstances and behaviour between mergers. They would hold that a single general prediction of the consequences of takeover is a will-o'-the-wisp; and their prescription would be that the state investigate thoroughly *each* prospective merger and decide on its particular merits whether it should be allowed to proceed.

But the resource cost of making such an examination in every case and of the subsequent monitoring necessary to see promises and commitments carried out, would be disproportionate given the level to which the merger rate sometimes rises: for instance, in 1968, over a hundred companies with a value of more than £500,000 each were taken over.[14] In such circumstances as these, a general presumption on the government's part for or against merger, could adequate grounds for forming it but be found, would seem to be an almost indispensable expedient. It will act as a filter: if the presumption is in favour, then only that minority of mergers which appears to pose marked difficulties for the public interest need be investigated thoroughly; if it is against, then only companies which believe that they can demonstrate net social benefits to be derived from the merger will present themselves for detailed examination.

And indeed state policy does harbour just such a presumption: that as a matter of fact mergers will do more good than harm — an attitude voiced in 1969 by the President of the Board of Trade: 'In general, mergers are desirable if they lead to better management or genuine economies of scale without eliminating workable competition. In my view, more often than not in Britain mergers will fulfil this condition.'[15] This presumption found expression in two areas of industrial policy. First, the Labour Government of the late sixties established the Industrial Reorganisation Corporation to promote some mergers.[16] Second, although the government possessed the power to investigate and prohibit a merger,[17] that power was but sparingly used: in that government's lifetime prospective mergers were referred to the Monopolies Commission at the rate of only two a year (and only half of these

---

14 See Department of Trade and Industry (1970)
15 Cited in George (1971), p. 155.
16 In the words of one of the I.R.C.'s members and supporters: 'The Corporation's principal purpose was to bring about mergers which would not otherwise have taken place . . . the case for the I.R.C. stands or falls on the propositions that in many sectors British companies were not large enough, and that without intervention they would not become large enough, soon enough.' (McClelland (1972)). The view was widespread in the sixties that European companies, and U.K. firms in particular, suffered a handicap of inadequate size relative to their American competitors — see Shonfield (1965), p. 74 and Servan Schreiber (1968). For a critical study of the proposition see Rowthorn (1971).
17 Under the Monopolies and Mergers Act, 1965.

were found to be against the public interest)[18] – an exceedingly low level when set against the flood of mergers at the time (documented above). Subsequently the attitude of those administering merger policy hardened somewhat: in 1973–4 the annual rate of reference to the Monopolies Commission reached 5. But still the guidelines for policy remained substantially unchanged: there persisted the presumption that the vast majority of takeovers were at the least not detrimental to the public interest and should proceed unchecked.[19]

The hypotheses

The chief measure of performance used to assess merger in this study is profitability, though other characteristics of acquiring companies are described and discussed in subsequent chapters. It might very well be asked, however, whether profitability is an adequate proxy for internal efficiency. True, some measure of profitability is conventionally used in a capitalist system as a performance index for particular firms; and indeed, other things equal, an improvement in the efficiency of a firm (defined, say, as a reduction in the resources actually used to produce a given output) will be sufficient for an improvement in profitability. But in a world of imperfect competition, oligopoly and monopoly, it cannot be maintained that an improvement in efficiency is *necessary* for a rise in profitability, and so the existence of the former cannot be inferred from evidence of the latter: profit gains could arise from improved bargaining power – at the expense of trading partners.

But this problem is not insuperable. For it may sometimes be reasonable to infer changes in efficiency from changes in profitability on the basis of expectations about changes in market power. For instance, suppose that it can be assumed that bargaining power is unchanged as a result of merger: then the other determinant of profitability change, alterations in efficiency, will dictate whether profitability rises, falls or remains unchanged.[20] Unless profitability rises, efficiency cannot be said to have improved. But the assumption of unchanged bargaining power is surely conservative: it is the very enhancement of the combine's market power which underlies the hostility to merger of one branch of *laissez-faire* economists, and which prompted the reservations over merger expressed by the President of the Board of Trade in the quotation above. And on the more plausible assumption that bargaining power has typically been enhanced by the merger, declines in efficiency can be inferred not just from reduced but also from unchanged profitability, whilst even improved profitability would now leave the efficiency conclusion indeterminate.

18 See Gribbin (1974).
   Under the 1965 Act the Board of Trade was empowered to refer to the Monopolies Commission any merger producing a market share for the combine of more than a third, or where the victim's assets exceeded £5 million in value. The subsequent Fair Trading Act (1973) reduced the market share threshold to 25%.
19 See Sir Geoffrey Howe (1973).
20 The efficiency change which may be inferred from a change in profitability on alternative assumptions about bargaining power can be represented in the following table:

	Bargaining power unchanged	Bargaining power increased
Profitability increased	↑	?
Profitability unchanged	0	↓
Profitability reduced	↓	↓

14

Granted, then, that some efficiency conclusions might be inferred from results for profitability alone, the ideal would be to compare the profitability achieved by a company after merger with the weighted average profitability that would have been achieved by the participant companies had the merger not taken place. The approximation to this ideal which has been attempted here consists of comparing the adjusted profitability achieved by the amalgamation after merger with an adjusted weighted average of the participants' profitability prior to merger.

Two types of adjustment have been made to the conventional measure of the firm's profitability in order to allow for systematic influences on profit other than merger, and hence to hold other things as near equal as possible. Firstly, allowance has been made for changes in the companies' environment during the period when profitability is measured. This is because the average level of profitability is known to vary with the trade cycle;[21] and some industries are known to be more sensitive than others to these cyclical fluctuations. At the same time, the level of merger activity has displayed a marked unevenness between years and between industries; so that, for reasons not directly associated with merger, years of numerous mergers may have been followed by years of above or below average profitability; and even if this has not been the pattern for the whole company sector, it could still have operated for some individual industries. A simple expedient has been adopted to 'remove' the external influence of the macro-economic and industry environment: expressing conventional profitability as a proportion of the current year's profitability of the industry in aggregate.[22] Where a company in one industry acquires a subsidiary from another, the yardstick adopted is a weighted average of the two industries' profitability, the weights being the proportionate contributions of each of the merging companies' net assets to the amalgamation's net assets.[23] The second step taken to hold other things equal has been to remove an accounting bias which frequently arises after takeover in the conventional measure of profitability. This occurs because acquirers often pay more for victims, and record the subsidiary's assets in their own books at a higher valuation, than the figure at which they appeared prior to takeover. This inflates the net assets of the amalgamation compared with the joint total of victim's and acquirer's net assets prior to merger (and had the merger not occurred), and so deflates the profitability measure (which has net assets as its denominator). Appendix A deals with this problem in greater detail, outlining the adjustment adopted below to yield an alternative profitability measure which should be largely free of this accounting bias.

Two complementary null hypotheses are tested:

I. that, other things equal, the profitability of the amalgamation is on average no different from the pre-merger level of the participants;

21 See, for example, Neild (1963). This observation is not necessarily in conflict with Cyert and March's propositions discussed above. Potential profit might rise in the upswing by much more than actual profit.
22 The aggregate rate of profit for the industry was obtained from Department of Industry (1971–5). The industry figure includes the companies under observation, so that differences between the companies studied and their industry figure will in general be smaller than those between the companies studied and the rest in their industry. Appendix C gives illustrative figures of average profit rates for industries over a seven-year period.
23 Because the data were not available for the actual date of merger, the weights were calculated for the end of the year preceding the merger.

15

II. that, other things equal, half of amalgamations experience an improvement in profitability after merger, and half a decline.

These can be expressed more precisely using the following symbols:

R: profitability
N: profit, after depreciation, but before tax
D: net assets
x: contribution (in terms of net assets) of victim to amalgamation
v: victim
q: acquirer
y: year of merger
u: victim's industry
w: acquirer's industry
j: a post-merger year (including year of merger)
z: amalgamation, when standardised
m: amalgamation (not standardised)
k: average of three pre-merger years
E: change in standardised profitability
H: change in standardised profitability, adjusted for accounting bias.

Profitability for any year, t, is defined as the profit flow during the year divided by the average net asset stock employed during the year:

$$R_t = \frac{2N_t}{D_{t-1} + D_t} \tag{3.i}$$

The weights used for the standardisation index are x, $(1-x)$, where

$$x = \frac{D_{v(y-1)}}{D_{q(y-1)} + D_{v(y-1)}} \tag{3.ii}$$

The actual standardisation index is, then, for any year, t:

$$xR_{ut} + (1-x)R_{wt} \tag{3.iii}$$

And the standardised profitability measure for the amalgamation in a post-merger year is:

$$R_{zj} = R_{mj} \div \{xR_{uj} + (1-x)R_{wj}\} \tag{3.iv}$$

This compares with standardised profitability for the base period:

$$R_{zk} = \frac{1}{3} \sum_{t=y-3}^{y-1} \left\{ \frac{2(N_{vt} + N_{qt})}{D_{v(t-1)} + D_{q(t-1)} + D_{vt} + D_{qt}} \div [xR_{ut} + (1-x)R_{wt}] \right\} \tag{3.v}$$

The pre-merger reference period is set at three years in order to summarise average performance over a run of years prior to the merger.[24] Hence, the crucial variable for this study, the change in profitability, is:

$$E_{zj} = R_{zj} - R_{zk} \qquad \text{(3.vi)}$$

And E is taken as the average value of E_{zj}, whilst H is the counterpart of E when R_{mj} (in 3.iv) has been adjusted for the accounting bias.

So the null hypotheses actually being tested can be summarised as:

I. $E = 0$; $H = 0$

II. $P = 0.5$; $Q = 0.5$; on the assumption that $E_{zj} = 0$ is an empty class; where P is the proportion of observations for which $E_{zj} < 0$, and Q is the proportion for which $H_{zj} < 0$.

Although the work is presented as formal statistical tests, there is a caveat over the interpretation that these tests may bear and on the population to which any results will apply, for the companies to be considered below are not, of course, a representative sample of all British companies (still less of all companies) for this period: rather, they are the larger British quoted companies; and many theories (especially the managerial ones) suggest that the objectives and behaviour of such firms might differ in important respects from those of their smaller brethren – in particular, quoted companies might well find the financing of takeover much easier than do non-quoted ones.[25] What is more, it is difficult to argue, given the evidence of chapter 2, that this study at least uses a representative sample of years drawn from the larger quoted British companies' long experience: the sample period witnessed unprecedentedly frenetic levels of takeover activity; and so it could be that the causes and consequences of takeovers in this period tended to differ from those of other periods.

The results are perhaps best seen as descriptions of the specific universe of larger British quoted companies which merged in the late sixties and early seventies.[26] Nevertheless, it is perhaps not unreasonable to presume, in the absence of contrary evidence, that the description which results may also apply to subsequent mergers among similar companies. The fact that Singh (1971) reported similar results for the fifties also encourages this presumption.

Despite these reservations, the statistical tests recorded still form a useful part of the description. They report the probability of a random process having generated the observed results; and the information they give on the relative dispersion of the

---

24 The choice of a three-year period is somewhat arbitrary. The longer the period the weaker the impact of temporary disturbances to profitability, but the more companies are excluded (on the grounds discussed below) because of a merger in the reference period. Three years was a pragmatic compromise.

It seems unlikely that the results would be very sensitive to the choice of reference period. If, for instance, the single year immediately before merger had been chosen instead, the declines in profitability from the reference level, recorded below, would have been greater, since, as appendix C shows, the 'amalgamation's' profitability was higher in that year than in either of the previous two.

25 See chapter 4 on the financing of takeover.

26 The question of whether the selection criteria detailed below produce an atypical subset even of these merging companies is taken up later.

observations can be a useful control on the interpretation of the averages that are provided in what follows.[27]

The takeovers selected for study

All the takeovers studied satisfy the following conditions:

1. The acquirer and the victim both belong to the population whose accounts are included in the Edinburgh Data Bank (see appendix B for details of the population).[28]

2. The takeovers took place between 1964 and 1972 (fuller details of takeovers were provided by the Department of Trade and Industry (D.I.) from 1964).[29]

3. Both acquirer and victim had at least three years' data available prior to the merger year (so that the reference level of profitability could be computed).

4. Neither victim nor acquirer took over any other quoted company in the pre-merger reference period. Where the acquirer took over another quoted company *after* the first merger, the study period for that acquirer is terminated in the year before the second merger; otherwise the acquirer's record is traced for every year until its death or the end of its record in the data bank. (This condition means that changes in performance can be more readily attributed to the single merger event.) Using these criteria, 233 acquisitions qualified for study. They represent rather over one-third of the cases of takeover of one quoted company[30] by another during this period.[31]

Of course, the length of the acquirer's record after merger varies from case to case: the numbers surviving and not acquiring for different periods after their initial acquisition are:

Year after merger	Number of acquirers' records still available in that year	Percentage of total acquirers' records studied still available
y	233	100.0
$y + 1$	211	91.7
$y + 2$	191	82.0
$y + 3$	161	69.1
$y + 4$	113	48.5
$y + 5$	73	31.3
$y + 6$	50	21.5
$y + 7$	23	9.9
$y + 8$	3	1.3

Where y = year of merger.

27 For instance, the relatively high dispersion of observations discovered below for the full set of observations, and reflected in the failure of differences in profitability to pass conventional tests of significance, acted as an alert to the fact that the means were unduly influenced by extreme observations.

28 Typically the takeovers studied involve only one victim; but when two or more victims from the same industry were taken over in the same year, their records were amalgamated, and they were treated as a single victim. There were five such cases.

29 Most of the other results presented in the book do not extend beyond 1971. This is because they require data for all companies in the data bank, which is currently available only until 1971. There was no objection to including in this particular study records for the minority of companies present in 1972.

30 Or, exceptionally, of more than one (see above).

31 Between 1964 and 1971 there were 596 cases of the takeover of one quoted company (exceptionally of more than one) by another. Of the takeovers studied, 223 fell within this period: the remaining 10 cases studied fell in 1972 when data for the full population are incomplete.

The number of acquirers surviving to successive post-merger years falls quite steeply. This is chiefly because no data are available in the data bank for any year after 1972 (and the data for 1972 only cover a minority of companies as yet: see appendix B), so that fewer than eight years post-merger data are available for any merger which took place after 1964 (and, of course, the later the merger, the fewer post-merger years are available). 68% of the records are terminated for this reason; 15% because the acquirer took over another company in a subsequent year and 13% because the acquirer was itself taken over; 3% because of exclusion from the population on the D.I's redefinition of membership criteria in 1969 (see appendix B); and the remaining 1% (Rolls Royce and Lines Bros) because of the appointment of a receiver. Thus the decline in the number of records available does *not* reflect a disastrous death rate among acquirers.

The pre-merger characteristics of victims and acquirers[32]

For each of the years 1964 to 1972, Table 3.A.I expresses the average size of those to become victims in the following year and of those to become acquirers in the following year as a percentage of the population average (for the full data bank) for this pre-merger year.[33] In every year the typical victim was a good deal smaller than the population average — less than half the size of the average member of the population in every year but one. The typical acquirer on the other hand was always bigger than average.[34] These results accord with the findings of Singh (1971) on the size of merger participants in the fifties.

The small size of the typical victim in relation to the amalgamation, implicit in the results above, was also calculated directly for each of the acquisitions studied: the net assets of the victim in the year preceding takeover were expressed as a percentage of the sum of the victim's and the acquirer's net assets in that year. The average value of this percentage was 25%. But this means that the merger still typically represented growth of around a third for the acquirer in the merger year, a figure which compares with a net asset growth rate of around 12% p.a. in this period for a typical member of the quoted company population.[35]

Table 3.A.II expresses, as an average, the profitability of victims and acquirers for each of the three years prior to the merger as a percentage of the profitability of their industry-year. The pooled average for the victims for the three pre-merger years is slightly greater than 100%: according to this criterion, the typical victim would appear to have performed slightly better than the industry. But the levels in all three years are very close to 100%: in no year is a difference recorded which is

32 This description applies not to the entire 233 cases selected above, but to a subset of 213, to which most of the subsequent analysis is confined: 20 cases with extreme observations were excluded at an early stage (see below).
33 The averages were computed from Department of Industry (1971–5). Since these population averages include the subset studied, the differences between these companies' records and the rest's will be greater still than the differences recorded here; and on a statistical test the difference between the sample average and the industry average might be rejected as insignificant in cases where the sample average would, if tested, have proved significantly different from that of the rest.
34 The percentages are lower for both groups after 1969 than before. This general decline is probably due not to an absolute fall in the size of participants but to the sharp rise in the average size of the D.I. population after the 1969 rebasing (see appendix B).
35 The net assets of the 966 continuing members of the population in the period 1964–71 grew by an average of 11.8% p.a. (see Table 2.B).

Table 3.A

I. The average size of those to become victims and those to become acquirers in the following year, as a percentage of the average for the D.I. quoted company population

Year of merger	Victim's size %	Acquirer's size %
1964	31	162
1965	42	376
1966	66	138
1967	33	175
1968	49	220
1969	45	140
1970	28	108
1971	18	104
1972	25	103

Note: net assets is used as the size measure.

II. The pre-merger profitability of victims and acquirers as a percentage of the profitability of the company's industry for that year

Year	Victim %	Acquirer %
$y - 3$	103.4	118.3[a]
	(43.8)	(47.1)
$y - 2$	104.0	124.9[a]
	(54.6)	(46.0)
$y - 1$	96.7	126.2[a]
	(66.9)	(48.9)

Notes: [a] Significantly different from 100% at the 1% level. The standard deviation appears in brackets beneath the mean.

y = year of merger.

Average profitability for the three years pooled:

Victim	Acquirer
101.4	123.1

See appendix C for the weighted average of both participants' profitability in the years before merger.

statistically significant at the 5% level. The typical victim may then be characterised as an average performer in terms of profitability. This is a description, however, that could not be applied to the typical acquirer, which, in contrast, out-performed its industry by a clear margin: its profitability was in the region of a quarter higher than average. Moreover, the dispersion of observations does not call into question this average result: in each year the acquirers' average profitability was significantly different from 100% at the stringent 1% level.[36] Again these conclusions bear out Singh's (1971 and 1975) findings on the pre-merger characteristics of merging companies: in particular the takeover mechanism does not appear to have singled

36 It is not certain that these conclusions can be taken as generalisations for the whole populations of victims and acquirers because the criteria on which the subset has been selected (see above) might have produced an atypical group of merger participants; but see the discussion below.

Table 3.B   The average change in standardised profitability after merger not adjusted for the accounting bias: all selected companies: with and without outliers

	I All cases				II Outliers omitted			
Year	E	S_e	P	n	E	S_e	P	n
y	0.038	3.179	0.378[c]	233	0.114[a]	0.105	0.371[c]	213
$y+1$	−0.168	2.158	0.582[c]	211	−0.053[a]	0.169	0.578[c]	192
$y+2$	−0.503	13.603	0.571	191	−0.035[b]	0.188	0.546	174
$y+3$	−0.369	4.942	0.565	161	−0.069[a]	0.236	0.541	146
$y+4$	−0.197	7.995	0.681[c]	113	−0.099[a]	0.237	0.670[c]	103
$y+5$	−0.567	10.590	0.658[c]	73	−0.109[a]	0.220	0.627[c]	67
$y+6$	−0.659	10.642	0.600	50	−0.068	0.236	0.545	44
$y+7$	−0.082	0.359	0.609	23	−0.073	0.316	0.619	21

Notes:
[a]   = Significantly different from 0 at the 1% level (using a t-test).
[b]   = Significantly different from 0 at the 5% level.
[c]   = Significantly different from 0.5 at the 5% level.
E = profitability of the amalgamation (standardised for industry and year) less 3-year average pre-merger profitability of the amalgamation (similarly standardised) (see definitions above).
S_e = standard deviation of E.
P = proportion of cases for which $E < 0$.
n = number of cases qualifying for inclusion in that year.
y = year of merger.

The average values of standardised profitability (R) for the two sets of amalgamations for each year are given in appendix C.

The results are not reported for the eighth year after merger, for which only three observations were available.

out the unprofitable as victims; and small size rather than low profitability appears to have been the characteristic which attracted the 'discipline' of takeover.

Post-merger performance: exploratory results
Section I of Table 3.B reports the typical change in the standardised profitability, before adjustment for the accounting bias, of the whole sample of selected amalgamations after merger, for each post-merger year. In the year of merger a slight improvement in profitability is typically recorded, with less than 40% of the sample recording a fall in the profitability measure used here;[37] but in all subsequent years an average decline is reported. The scale of the decline is considerable, amounting in some years to more than half the level of profitability achieved by the industry. However, the dispersion of values for the change in profitability, reflected in the standard deviation of E, is enormous in comparison with the mean; and consequently the change is in no year significantly different from zero at the 5% level.[38]

37 But see below on the measurement problems which affect results for the year of merger.
38 Nevertheless, the nonparametric statistic P, the proportion of amalgamations showing a decline in profitability, which is not sensitive to outlying observations, confirms that a majority did display a decline, the proportion which did being in some years significantly different from 0.5 at the 5% level.

Given the large standard deviation of E, it seemed possible that the estimate of E's average was heavily influenced by a small number of extreme observations. If this were so, and if those extreme values were due to special factors unconnected with merger, then the averages reported could be misleading indicators of the effect of merger on profitability. Ideally, outliers would be excluded where prior knowledge was available that their extreme values reflected special circumstances. Such detailed knowledge of the characteristics of individual members of this sample was not available, however; and an expedient was adopted here of excluding cases where any individual observation of E exceeded a predetermined, but arbitrary limit. This was set at a change in profitability greater than 200% of the level recorded by the industry; and it involved the exclusion of 20 of the original 233 cases.[39]

As Section II of Table 3.B shows, the results with the outliers removed are much weaker in terms of the absolute value of the change (the mean decline is much smaller), but much stronger in terms of statistical significance (the dispersion of observations is much smaller and the null hypothesis of no change in profitability is rejected at the 1% level in five years, and at the 5% level in a further year). The proportions experiencing declines in profitability are little affected by the exclusion of outliers (see the note on this statistic above): it remains true that, in all years but the actual year of merger, the majority experience a decline, and that this majority is statistically significant in four years. In subsequent comparisons it is assumed that the exclusion of outliers is justified, and attention is confined to the reduced set of 213 amalgamations.

Whether or not outliers are excluded, however, the results display a curious discontinuity: whilst the merger-year typically shows an improvement in profitability, every subsequent year witnesses a decline from the pre-merger level. As there are known to be particular problems in calculating profitability for the actual year of merger, it could be that an explanation of this feature is to be found

---

39 In fact the plea of special case can be sustained with prior evidence for a sizeable minority of the companies excluded: 5 belonged to the shipbuilding industry whose average profitability was so low in some years of the period (see the averages reported in appendix C) that quite small absolute changes in R_{mj} (see 3.iv) would result in very big changes in the standardised measure, R_{zj}, and hence in E_{zj}. The experience of these companies would then be magnified to have a quite disproportionate effect on the mean of E.

The proportion of 'failures' among these extreme cases in some ways resembles that for the set of mergers with outliers omitted:

Year	Percentage recording decline in profitability
y	40
$y + 1$	58
$y + 2$	76
$y + 3$	73
$y + 4$	80
$y + 5$	100
$y + 6$	100
$y + 7$	50

Thus these extreme cases do not display records qualitatively different from those of the rest, but simply magnify the change reported, and have an unduly large impact on the averages across all cases.

in them.[40] Had the two companies not merged, their weighted average profitability in the merger-year (R^*_{my}) would have been (see above):

$$R^*_{my} = \frac{N_{qy} + N_{vy}}{\frac{1}{2}(D_{q(y-1)} + D_{v(y-1)} + D_{qy} + D_{vy})} \qquad \text{(3.vii)}$$

i.e. twelve months' profit flow for each participant divided by the average net asset stock for the two participants together. Exactly the same terms for the acquirer (q) are included in the actual profitability formula for the amalgamation (which, by convention, is based on the acquirer's accounts); but since the victim was not part of the amalgamation at the beginning of the year, *its* opening net assets do not appear in the denominator; whilst in the numerator there appears, on the victim's side, just the profit for whatever number of months the victim has belonged to the amalgamation.[41] If s is the proportion of the year for which the victim has contributed to the amalgamation's profit, then the profitability measure derived from the acquirer's accounts will be:

$$R_{my} = \frac{N_{qy} + sN_{vy}}{\frac{1}{2}(D_{q(y-1)} + D_{qy} + D_{vy})} \qquad \text{(3.viii)}$$

How does the use of R to represent R^* affect the picture? In one extreme case the outcome is clear: if the merger took place at the beginning of the parent's financial year $(s = 1)$, then R would exceed R^* (the numerator being the same for the two measures, but the denominator of R being smaller by $\frac{1}{2}D_{v(y-1)}$). For values of s less than 1, however, the outcome will depend on the actual values of the profit and net asset figures: it becomes possible that R would fall short of R^*, but still R *could* exceed R^*, even at the opposite polar case where $s = 0$.[42] And in fact, if plausible average values are substituted in (3.vii) and (3.viii), it turns out that s would have to be less than 0.5 to bring R and R^* into equality.[43] Or, expressing this slightly differently, were mergers distributed evenly through the year (so that average $s = 0.5$), then the average of R, the observed value, will exceed that of R^*, the 'true' value.[44]

40 A further possibility is that acquiring companies indulge heavily in 'window dressing' in the year of merger to reassure shareholders of the fruits of the merger. This would involve using any discretion enjoyed by the management in assessing profit to over- rather than under- state earnings (e.g. in the valuation of stocks and in the selection of bad and doubtful debts).

41 Of course, the other side of this coin is that the victim's pre merger accounting period may often not be a year; but distortion is avoided on this account because the D.I. scales the records up or down to an equivalent for a twelve month period.

42 For example, substitute in (3.vii) the following values:

$$R^* = \frac{10 + 2}{\frac{1}{2}(10 + 20 + 10 + 20)} = 0.4$$

Then,

$$R = \frac{10}{\frac{1}{2}(10 + 10 + 20)} = 0.5$$

43 If the victim's profitability were 16%, the acquirer's 20% and the victim were one-third the size of the acquirer, then s would need to be 0.43 to bring R and R^* into equality. These values are taken from the averages for the mergers studied, which are reported above.

44 Barring perverse results because of systematic differences between the records of companies merging early in the year and the experience of those merging later.

In the absence of either *a priori* considerations or evidence to the contrary it might seem reasonable to assume that the mergers being studied occurred at a constant rate through the year and hence that, with s averaging 0.5, R has been inflated. However, as the inter-year comparisons of chapter 2 showed, the merger rate was certainly not uniform *between* years — rather, merger activity progressed by fits and starts. The same may well have been true within years; and just one burst of merger activity in the first half of a single year, with the merger rate at all other times uniform, would have been sufficient to raise R a good deal further above R^*. Equally, of course, this unpredictable distortion could have worked in the opposite direction, partially offsetting the systematic upward bias in R or perhaps even causing R to fall below R^*. But the subsequent record of the amalgamations makes it seem unlikely that the bias in fact went this way: after all, in *every* later year the typical amalgamation experienced a decline in its standardised profitability. And it is difficult to see why gains in productive efficiency or market power which did boost profitability in the year of purchase would typically not only be eliminated but actually be reversed at the end of the year of merger.[45]

Given unlimited resources, one would settle this issue by adjusting each amalgamation's profitability for the merger year to remove any distortion. But the clerical effort of doing this would in practice be disproportionate, involving detailed study of the participants' published accounts — and it has not been attempted here. Still, the systematic bias in R on the neutral assumption about timing, together with the potentially significant but capricious distortion which an irregular timing pattern can produce, certainly call into question the exceptional results for the year of merger. Accordingly, in the results and conclusions which follow, it is the unanimous results for all post-merger years which are emphasised, whilst the record for the actual merger year is mentioned but given relatively little weight.

Post-merger performance: principal results

The previous section has cleared the ground for the principal results which are presented in Table 3.C. Section I of the table duplicates section II of Table 3.B, giving the average change in merely standardised profitability with outliers removed. Section II provides the corresponding results when profitability is adjusted for the pervasive accounting bias afflicting asset valuations after merger (discussed above and dealt with more fully in appendix A). Now, that appendix fosters the expectation that adjusted post-merger profitability will be higher than the unadjusted version, and hence that, on the adjusted basis, improvements in profitability will be all the greater, with apparent declines mitigated or even reversed. This expectation is borne out by the results: in the event, the improvement formerly recorded in the year of merger is enhanced; and while the subsequent declines are in no year reversed, in several they are smaller.[46] Consequently, the null hypothesis of no

---

45 It is possible, but again unlikely, that it was the companies which did not 'survive' to $y + 1$ which were outstandingly successful in y, and tipped the balance, to yield an average improvement for all cases.

46 $y + 5$ actually shows a slightly larger decline. This can arise under the estimation procedure detailed in appendix A when the acquiring company chooses to write off goodwill already existing in the victim's balance sheet. This reversal of the usual bias is, however, likely to be of minor proportions and relatively infrequent (see Lee (1974)).

Table 3.C The average change in standardised profitability: before and after adjustment for the accounting bias (outliers omitted)

Year	I Unadjusted profitability				II Adjusted profitability			
	E	S_e	P	n	H	S_h	P	n
y	0.114[a]	0.105	0.371[c]	213	0.148[a]	0.106	0.338[c]	213
$y+1$	−0.053[a]	0.169	0.578[c]	192	−0.015	0.172	0.536	192
$y+2$	−0.035[b]	0.188	0.546	174	−0.010	0.192	0.517	174
$y+3$	−0.069[a]	0.236	0.541	146	−0.058[a]	0.237	0.527	146
$y+4$	−0.099[a]	0.237	0.670[c]	103	−0.098[a]	0.234	0.660[c]	103
$y+5$	−0.109[a]	0.220	0.627[c]	67	−0.110[a]	0.220	0.642[c]	67
$y+6$	−0.068	0.236	0.545	44	−0.067	0.235	0.523	44
$y+7$	−0.073	0.316	0.619	21	−0.073	0.316	0.619	21

Notes:
[a] Significantly different from 0 at the 1% level.
[b] Significantly different from 0 at the 5% level.
[c] Significantly different from 0.5 at the 5% level.

E = as defined in Table 3.B.
H = profitability of the amalgamation (standardised for industry and year and adjusted for the accounting bias) less 3-year average pre-merger profitability of the amalgamation (similarly standardised) (see definition above).
S = standard deviation.
P = proportion of cases for which E and H respectively <0.
n = number of cases qualifying for inclusion in that year.
y = year of merger.

The average values of standardised profitability (R and F respectively) for each year are given in appendix C.

difference is no longer rejected on the usual statistical test in years $y+1$ and $y+2$ as it was when the unadjusted measure was used. But though the estimated size of the change in profitability is in most cases changed, still the qualitative conclusion of the earlier sections can rest unamended. Every year after merger reveals a decline in profitability; in three years this decline is significantly different from zero at the 1% level; and in each post-merger year the majority of companies experience a decline. True, the result for the actual merger year still runs counter to the rest; but given the potential distortion which might afflict the figures for that year, too much significance should not be attached to this exception. In general, then, it can be said that a mild decline in profitability did typify these mergers. On the arguments presented above, if market power was typically unchanged as a result of the merger, the profitability decline reflects a fall in efficiency. And if, as seems plausible, market power was more often enhanced by merger, then the profitability decline is likely to understate the loss in efficiency.

A possible criticism of the principal results and an alternative cross-section approach

One potential objection to the universality of this conclusion lies in the special nature of the mergers studied here, given the criteria used in their selection (see above). These criteria were adopted so that the impact of the single merger event might be traced over a series of years; and they caused some companies which were heavily engaged in takeover to be excluded. An alternative approach to assessing the impact of takeover upon profitability (and one which might offer further evidence on differences between single, or at any rate infrequent, and intensive acquisition) would be to estimate a relationship between profitability and the rate of growth by takeover across companies — that is, to ask to what extent companies growing more rapidly than average by takeover are more or less profitable than average — instead of comparing profitability before and after takeover as in the earlier sections.

This alternative exercise is, however, immediately confronted by problems of interpretation: would, say, a positive association between takeover and profitability mean that companies were more profitable because they were taking over more or that they were able to take over more because they were more profitable? It is the former direction of causation — from takeover to profitability — which has been at issue in this chapter; but there are theoretical grounds for expecting strong forces to be working in the opposite direction. The reasons why the ability to grow (by whatever means) might be expected to depend positively on profitability are enumerated more fully in chapter 4: other things equal, more profit yields more savings available for reinvestment and makes both management and the capital market willing to entertain the provision of more external finance.

This relationship between profitability and the rate of growth that can be financed is what Marris (1964) has represented in a 'finance limit curve'. It appears as one element (the straight line) in the diagram he uses to summarise the mutual dependence of the growth and profit rates: this diagram is reproduced in figure 3.A. The other element is termed a 'demand growth curve' by Marris, and depicts the maximum profitability attainable at any rate of growth. This second element is, of course, the relationship which would incorporate the effects of growth by merger upon profitability. In Marris' version it is supposed to have an inverted U-shape: this growth—profitability relation is reckoned to be positive in the lower range of growth rates but negative in the upper, for reasons given in an earlier section of this chapter.

A number of writers[47] have argued that a scatter of observations on the growth and profit rates of a set of firms will approximate not the 'demand growth curve' but the 'finance limit curve'. This is because all (or at least all quoted) firms are reckoned to face a common capital market which will set a common limit on the rate of growth of capital which may be achieved for a given rate of profit (chapter 4 discusses the arguments on this issue in more detail). Two mutually dependent ratios will determine this limit: the proportion of profit that is retained (retention ratio) and the quantity of external finance that the market will subscribe on acceptable terms as a proportion of current profit (matching ratio). Other things equal, a higher retention ratio (at the cost of dividends), though permitting more expansion from savings, will lose market favour and depress the feasible matching ratio. And given the market's relative preference for current (dividend) as opposed to future income, there will exist some combination of retention and matching ratios which will maximise the rate of growth attainable by any firm for a given rate of profit. As against this, the forces operating to make profitability depend upon growth in

47 For example, Marris (1964), Singh and Whittington (1968) and Whittington (1971).

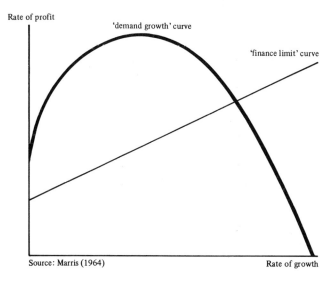

Rate of profit

'demand growth' curve

'finance limit' curve

Source: Marris (1964)

Rate of growth

Figure 3.A. The mutual dependence of the rate of growth and the rate of profit: one possible pair of relationships.

an *identical* way for different firms are judged rather weak.[48] Many factors affecting the force of this relationship seem likely to vary considerably among firms: management ability; inherited products and equipment; the flow of new products and techniques from research and development programmes; the penetration of foreign markets, etc.

This study follows the conventional argument in attributing the observed statistical association between growth and profitability to the finance relationship (profitability the explanatory variable) which is believed relatively stable across firms and which is identified by the variability of the 'demand growth curve'.[49] This means, of course, that the observed cross-section association between profitability and growth by takeover cannot be taken as an indicator of the impact of takeover upon profitability (the principal issue in this chapter) and that causal inferences must be confined to the finance relationship, the topic considered in chapter 4.

48 In the case of growth by takeover, support for this proposition is provided by the appendix to this chapter. There it appears that, surprisingly, the extent of the decline in profitability after takeover does not bear a clear systematic relationship to the size of the victim (as a proportion of the acquirer's size).
49 If firms operate within the potential boundaries (because of ignorance or the failure to realise potential achievements which Cyert and March or Leibenstein emphasise) then the scatter of observations will be located rather above the finance limit curve: the intercept may be higher but the slope need be no different from the 'underlying' relationship.

Table 3.D   The pre-tax profitability of companies with different rates of growth by takeover, 1948–64 and 1964–71

Classification according to rate of growth by acqui-sition	1948–64		1964–71	
	Number of companies	Profitability % p.a.	Number of companies	Profitability % p.a.
Zero	202	18.6	188	19.2
Low	524	17.6	388	16.1
Appreciable	424	17.9	290	17.0
High	524	18.0	390	18.1
Intensive	100	18.4	100	21.2
Overall average	1250	17.9	966	17.5

Notes:

Profitability is defined, as elsewhere in the chapter, as pre-tax profit divided by average net assets.

In each case the figure reported is the average of annual profit rates across all company-years within a group-period.

For full details of the companies within these groups, see appendix D. 'Appreciable' and 'Intensive' are subgroups of 'High'.

Whilst I find this reasoning convincing, however, some might dispute this resolution of the identification problem and might even go as far as reversing the argument, maintaining that no uniform 'finance limit' relationship exists, but that, instead, it is growth's influence on profitability which is common to firms and dominates the observed association. Some estimates of the cross-section relationship between profitability and growth by takeover are therefore provided in Table 3.D. for those who would subscribe to this alternative view. This table analyses the population of continuing quoted companies[50] into four categories which are used again at several points below. One category contains those which undertook no expenditure on subsidiaries during the respective period.[51] The rest are ranked according to their rate of growth by takeover and the bottom half allocated to the 'low' group,[52] while the other half, the 'high' group is further subdivided into two categories, the top 100 by growth by acquisition ('intensive' acquirers) and the rest ('appreciable' acquirers). A non-linear pattern emerges in both the periods covered (1948–64 and 1964–71): the profitability performance of the middling groups (low and appreciable) was mediocre — less than or equal to the overall average; whilst the intensive group was more profitable, roughly matching the zero group in the earlier period

50 See appendix B for the full definition of these populations.
51 These comparisons might be thought to suffer from the drawback that no allowance is made for the systematic influence of industry, a factor which is taken into account explicitly in the single merger study above and in the discussion of finance below.
52 The low group's typical member achieved only trivial growth by acquisition: the group averages for this variable were only 0.1% p.a. and 0.3% p.a. for 1948–64 and 1964–71 respectively, and the maximum values achieved by any member of the group were 0.9% and 2.2% respectively. Given the Department of Industry's method of deriving this figure, these trivial levels of growth by acquisition might represent not just the infrequent acquisition of relatively small subsidiaries, but also piecemeal purchases of shares which do not necessarily yield full control over other companies; or perhaps the net outcome of purchases and sales of subsidiaries.

and excelling it in the later one.[53] Thus in the event these figures not only defy a universally acceptable interpretation but also elude very simple description: further discussion of them, in the context of financing takeover, comes in the next chapter.

After this protracted discussion of the merits of applying cross-section analysis to the issue of the gains from merger, it still remains to be demonstrated that the single merger study of this chapter does not systematically neglect those acquiring companies which were most successful at assimilating new subsidiaries and which were therefore particularly willing to rely heavily on growth by acquisition. In fact a number of defences are available against this criticism, without recourse to cross-section analysis. Firstly, the set of acquirers studied is actually well represented among the companies enjoying rapid rates of growth by takeover. If the 966 members of the total population of companies which continued from 1964 to 1971 are ranked according to their rate of growth by takeover, then 38% of the top 100 are included in the study reported above, as are 32% of those ranked below 100 but above the median, compared with only 9% of those in the bottom half of the ranking by growth by takeover.[54] Still, shifting his ground, the sceptic might argue that those which were highly ranked according to this procedure but which also qualified for inclusion in this single merger study do not *typify* intensive acquirers – they earned their high ranking with a single very large takeover (in relation to their own size) or a small number of them; whereas it could be that companies which achieve rapid growth by frequent but *small* (and hence more easily assimilated) takeovers enjoy more success. But appendix A gives no comfort to this view either: very large takeovers (in this relative sense) were not markedly less successful than smaller ones, despite *a priori* expectations to the contrary.

It is not necessarily the case, of course, that companies which fail to realise efficiency gains in one merger will subsequently abstain from others (and that

53 The accounting bias discussed at length above and in appendix A needs to be borne in mind here of course: companies growing more rapidly by takeover are likely to have a bigger proportion of goodwill arising on consolidation in their balance sheet. And it might be argued that this unduly deflates their profitability, distorting any comparison. In the comparisons made above, of post- with pre-merger performance for a given amalgamation, this accounting feature *would* distort the comparison, and adjustment has been made, but in cross-section comparisons it is not clear that the valuation excluding goodwill will always be appropriate: depending on the yardstick being used, a current rather than historic valuation may be preferable.

Nevertheless, alternative measures have been calculated, for completeness. For all the companies, profitability was recomputed with all goodwill deducted from the net assets denominator. This is, of course, a crude expedient, since not all goodwill arises on the consolidation of new subsidiaries. The alternative profitability measure took on the following values:

	1948–64	1964–71
Zero	19.1	19.7
Low	18.5	16.7
Appreciable	18.7	18.5
High	19.1	20.1
Intensive	20.6	24.7

The result, then, is qualitatively similar: the nonlinearity persists. But the acquiring companies appear in a somewhat more favourable light.

54 For full details of the overlap, see Table D.L in appendix D. The overlap with the intensive acquirers will arise not only if the single merger is very big, but also when some years' experience of one of the mergers of an active acquirer qualify for inclusion.

repeated merger will be a sign of success). For efficiency gains may never have been a motive for the merger in the first place (see the theoretical discussion above and below). Or else, although efficiency gains were sought in the first merger, the acquirer might resemble the gentleman who had been very unhappy in marriage, and yet married again immediately after his wife died – prompting Dr Johnson's remark that 'it was the triumph of hope over experience'.

A further counter to the objection that the selection procedure biasses the results draws upon a complementary study of U.K. takeovers in the sixties by Utton (1974). There Utton compares the profitability performance of a merger-intensive group during and after a heavy bout of takeover activity for each company with that of a group which relied instead on internal growth. The merging companies' average profitability was appreciably below that of the non-merging companies, too far below to be readily explained by any of the measurement problems presented by the exercise (and acknowledged by Utton).[55] Thus Utton's study, deliberately framed to capture the consequences of a series of takeovers by a company, yields results in full harmony with those reported above for the single merger case.

Relation of the results with earlier work

It has already been suggested that the two studies of mergers in the United Kingdom which test similar hypotheses to those adopted here both concur in this chapter's chief conclusion, that there is no evidence that merger enhanced profitability, which, on the contrary, was by and large unfavourably affected. Utton's (1974) study has just been cited at the end of the previous section, and Singh (1971) found that a majority of amalgamations experienced a decline in profitability after merger.[56]

Further corroboration of these results comes from studies of company size and performance. Just as it is difficult to find evidence that the process of achieving greater size by merger typically enhanced profitability, so also it is hard to find a study showing that a greater initial endowment of size (whether achieved by internal or external means) is generally associated with a profit rate above average. Almost without exception, U.K. studies reveal either no systematic relationship or else a weak inverse relationship between size and profitability.[57] It may seem to some that these results sit oddly with evidence of potential economies of scale.

55 Two principal objections might be raised to Utton's results. First, they do not take explicit account of the influence of industry on differences in profitability, though there is no clear expectation of a bias here. And second, they do not make allowance for the accounting bias discussed in appendix A. But the accounting bias would have to be very big to explain away his observed differences: for instance, if, on average, the victim's book value at the time of merger represented a third of the amalgamation's book value at the end of the period, goodwill equivalent to 40% of the victim's net assets would have to have been incorporated to explain away the difference. The average ratio of goodwill to victim's net assets never reached this level in the years studied in appendix A.
56 Appendix B discusses results for studies in other countries.
57 See Samuels and Smyth (1968); Singh and Whittington (1968), Ch. 6; Whittington (1971), ch. 3; Meeks and Whittington (1975b); Meeks and Whittington (1976), section 3. One recent study (Smyth, Boyes and Peseau (1975)) found that although profitability was negatively related to size on most measures of size, when the stock market valuation of the firm's equity was used as a size measure, the negative relationship did not result. This does not necessarily contradict the earlier results on the influence of size upon profitability, however, since this particular size measure is likely itself to be influenced by profitability: other things equal, a more profitable firm will be expected to enjoy a higher market valuation.

But, of course, the theoretical approaches reviewed above, emphasising the inertia of aspirations and the development of 'organisational slack' help to reconcile evidence of potential gains with the absence of any actual improvement in performance as size increases. And indeed, evidence has appeared of some symptoms of ailments which might afflict large organisations — however promising their performance might be in engineering terms. It appears that bigger plants suffer worse strike records;[58] and there is evidence that they also suffer more accidents per man and enjoy less favourable utilisation of their labour force on account of absenteeism and sickness.[59]

Further, two studies with an approach very different from that adopted here provide complementary findings on the experience of takeovers. Both are based on the more detailed study of relatively small numbers of companies rather than on the more anonymous assessment of a far larger group. First, the case study treatment of mergers in particular markets by Hart, Utton and Walshe (1973) revealed evidence of managerial diseconomies following merger (p. 101 to 102). Second, Newbould (1970) used evidence from interviews with the managers of acquiring companies, coupled with published financial information on these firms: he arrives at the conclusion that 'management appears to be the only consistent gainer from merger activity' (p. 193). And, in fact, one way in which managers might benefit financially from merger, even if profitability suffered as a result of the merger, can be illustrated by combining the results of this chapter with those of an earlier paper (Meeks and Whittington (1975a)) on the relationship of directors' pay to performance, to yield estimates of the likely overall effect on directors' pay of the typical merger studied here.

That earlier paper argued, against the majority of earlier studies, that the influence of profitability on director's pay is not trivial, but it is in agreement with earlier work in according a major role to size. Table 3.E uses the estimates of the earlier paper and of this chapter to assess the likely impact on salary of the gain in size and loss in profitability associated with the typical merger. The method of, and problems in, predicting pay changes through time from cross-section regression estimates are discussed in the earlier paper; and while the results should not be interpreted too precisely, Table 3.E suggests that the increase in pay which followed the growth implied by the typical merger studied here would far outweigh the decrease in pay which the regression estimates would predict because of the resulting decline in profitability. If these estimates are to be trusted, the highest paid director would gain a net pay rise of over £1000 p.a. as a result of the typical merger studied here. In other words, while the typical merger may well have been to the detriment of the collective shareholders of the victim and acquirer, it would yield appreciable salary benefits to the amalgamation's directors.

Last but not least, the Monopolies Commission provides some evidence on the economies which participants expected from merger. Sutherland, an analyst of the Commission's reports, concluded that 'the net savings, when they are quantified at all, are . . . rather strikingly small'.[60] But even these trifling savings were only

58 See Department of Employment (1976), bearing in mind the qualifications in Wigham (1976).
59 See Taylor (1976) and Revans (1960).
60 Sutherland (1969), p. 66. This conclusion was endorsed in a subsequent study of more recent Monopolies Commission investigations by Utton (1975).

Table 3.E   The impact of the average takeover on the salary of the highest paid
director

Averages of the estimates provided in Meeks and Whittington (1975a) suggest
that a unit difference in the natural log of size[a] was associated with a difference of
£4204 in pay;[b] and that a difference of one percentage point in the rate of return
was associated with a difference of £89 in pay.

The typical merger reported in chapter 3 represented growth of one-third for the
acquirer, which corresponds to an increase of 0.285 in the natural log of size.

It produced, according to chapter 3, a decline in profitability of about 7% of the
industry-year level. Taking the industry-year level as about 15% (roughly the average for the D.I. quoted company population (see Department of Industry 1971–5)),
this implies a decline of roughly 1.05 percentage points.

Thus:

Gain on merger = 0.285 × £ 4204	= £	1198
Loss on merger = 1.05 × £ 89	= £	93
Net gain on merger	= £	1105

Notes:
[a] When net assets are used as the size measure: see annex to Meeks and Whittington (1975a).
[b] When the salary of the highest paid director is used as the measure of pay.

notional expected ones at best and were in some cases disputed by the Commission
– and anyway, as was seen above, some theories of the firm outlined earlier would
predict that, especially if the merger weakened competitive pressures on management, any such potential gains might never be translated into enhanced overall
efficiency, being absorbed in greater organisational slack instead.[61] It is true that
the Commission examines a biassed sample from the population of prospective
mergers – those which, given the past presumption in favour of allowing merger,
the government's initial screening process has selected as requiring further study
before they can be sanctioned. But since the explicit criteria for reference are size
and market share, rather than the lack of prospective efficiency gains, it is not
necessarily the case that the mergers which went through without referral offered
more substantial potential economies than those which were examined by the
Commission.

Summary and conclusions

Two groups of *laissez-faire* economists with conflicting views on merger
were distinguished. The one maintains that merger undermines the competitive
conditions which are required if *laissez-faire* is to achieve allocative efficiency
within markets and productive efficiency within firms. The second argues against
state interference in the merger process: not only is *any* state intervention objection-
able on political grounds, but also economic grounds are cited for the belief that
mergers will be in the public interest. Why, some of these economists ask, would a
firm ever bother to buy another if merging did not pay? And does not the evidence
that scale economies are to be had in many British industries provide a sound reason
for expecting merger to pay?

61 See the discussion above of behavioural theories and *X* efficiency.

In contrast, a number of modern developments in the theory of the firm, which abandon the *laissez-faire* framework, stressing the permissiveness of markets and the preponderance of managerial rather than owner control, prompt a less sanguine view. Again characterising these theories only very crudely, the one branch suggests that the performance of very many firms falls below their potential and that improvements in potential (cost reductions or improved bargaining terms) brought about by merger might elicit no enhancement of performance, but instead permit an easier life for management. The second branch suggests that the pattern of incentives might induce managers to pursue the company's growth even at the expense of profitability.

The clash of theoretical views demands a resolution – not least, it was argued, because judging each case on its merits is an expensive procedure for the state in years of intense merger activity: in fact the presumption has prevailed that merger *will* further the public interest, detailed scrutiny being reserved for a very small minority of prospective amalgamations. In default of agreement on *a priori* grounds, the core of the chapter attempted an empirical resolution of the issue, comparing the profitability experience of a large group of amalgamations which were formed in the sixties and early seventies with the pre-merger record of the participants. The significant finding was that in all the seven post-merger years which were observed, on average profitability showed a decline from the pre-merger level. This result held whether or not outlying observations were included; before and after adjustment for the known accounting bias; and (as the appendix to this chapter shows) almost without exception for diverse sub-groups of mergers segregated according to their degree of diversification or the size of the victim in relation to the acquirer. In many of these cases the decline was statistically significant at the 1% or 5% levels. Admittedly, the typical decline was not enormous (for all results without outliers it was only once more than 10% of the industry level) and reservations must remain over experience in the year of merger. Nevertheless, on the weak neutral assumption that market power was unchanged as a result of the merger, efficiency would seem to have suffered after merger. And on the more plausible assumption that profitability should probably receive a fillip through merger from enhanced market power, the profitability loss will be an underestimate of the loss in internal efficiency.[62]

Complementary evidence from other writers was cited in support of these findings. This included Monopolies Commission investigations reporting the trifling expected economies from merger claimed by the participants, and earlier studies showing that merger had actually had an unfavourable impact on profitability. In addition, the available evidence suggested that while greater size might often appear to offer potential economies, in practice it was associated with worse strike records, worse absenteeism, more accidents and more days per man lost through illness, but *not* higher profitability.

Thus these results accord ill with the expectations of *laissez-faire* adherents of free merger: even if expected gains in efficiency were the usual motive for merger,

---

62 This leaves aside any adverse effects from the merger upon the allocative efficiency of markets when competition is weakened, a consequence which looms large in the fear of many *laissez-faire* opponents of free merger.

it appears that typically they were not realised.[63] The alternative behavioural and growth theories of the firm could yield the observed outcome, however: the typical efficiency loss after merger is entirely consistent with the inertia of aspirations, the pursuit of a quiet life or the sacrifice of profitability to growth. Indeed, an earlier section of the chapter suggested that, judging by evidence of the average influence of growth and profitability upon directors' pay, managers with no ownership interest in the firm would typically have benefited from higher salaries as a result of the average merger studied here, even though profitability was impaired. This is quite apart from the range of other benefits which accrue to managers from merger. As was argued above, these include the elimination of competitive pressure and the gain of greater power and prestige. In addition, earlier studies have shown that, other things equal, greater size typically brings a company more stable performance and greater immunity from being taken over itself, and hence the quieter life for management that some suggest they seek.[64]

Thus the behavioural and growth theories would prompt no general expectation of social gains following merger and provide no basis for a state presumption in favour of merger; indeed, as a step towards a quieter life or growth for its own sake, merger might well, on their argument, be detrimental to efficiency. Then, among the more conventional theorists, one branch argues for an outright ban on a major class of mergers on the grounds that it weakens the competitive pressures which are believed to safeguard productive and allocative efficiency. Only the second branch of *laissez-faire* economists argues positively in favour of free merger; but even these, like the President of the Board of Trade quoted above, have felt the need to hedge their expectations of efficiency gains with reservations about merger's impact upon competition. For instance, the authors of a study of scale economies circumscribed their advocacy of greater company size, to achieve the potential economies of scale which they had documented, with fears for the survival of competition:[65]

> 'Where there is a long-run conflict between the maintenance of competition and the full achievement of economies of scale . . . it is difficult to assess the best compromise between scale and competition . . . it is possible to make estimates of the economies of scale, but it would be very difficult to assess the impact on the efficiency of an industry of the presence or absence of competition.'

Again, a member and enthusiastic supporter of the government body set up to

63 Might the observed behaviour still represent profit maximisation? It does not appear to be consistent with profit maximisation in conditions of perfect competition, since under such circumstances a transfer of control leading to a less efficient utilisation of resources would be inhibited. But, then, the very existence of scale economies (for some, the *raison d'être* of merger activity) undermines the conditions of perfect competition. Outside perfect competition, the observed behaviour could represent profit maximisation. For instance, where an imperfect capital market gave a potential victim too low a valuation taking into account its current and potential performance, a profit-maximising acquirer might be induced to buy it – notwithstanding expectations of efficiency losses compared with the situation had the two not merged.
64 It is not necessarily the case that British managers have achieved a quieter life after their intensive merger activity than they enjoyed before it. Simultaneous developments, such as legislation outlawing restrictive practices and the liberalisation of world trade, may well have been working in the opposite direction. But life will still, on these arguments, have become quieter than it would have been in the absence of merger.
65 Pratten, Dean and Silberston (1965), p. 105.

promote merger, the Industrial Reorganisation Corporation, voiced a related qualification:[66]

> 'Even where it can be established that mergers would enable economies of scale to be exploited, it is necessary to consider whether such an advantage would not be more than offset by a reduced intensity of competition, leading to prices being raised against the consumer and to a misallocation of resources.'

But since the supposed gains from merger are not typically forthcoming, only the qualifications remain.[67] With the pragmatic justification of free merger — that it works — denied, the diverse theoretical objections would seem to demand that the state's presumption in favour of merger be reversed.

APPENDIX TO CHAPTER 3

Chapter 3 described the typical pattern of profitability after merger for all the companies studied. This appendix asks whether the pattern varies between particular subsets of these companies. If so, detailed government scrutiny could perhaps be directed at limited subsets of mergers whose performance has typically been poor in the past. On the basis of theoretical arguments two criteria are adopted here for distinguishing between sets of mergers: whether the victim is from the same, an allied, or an entirely different industry; and the size of the victim in relation to that of the acquirer.

Diversification and post-merger performance

Introduction

The diversified merger prompts conflicting considerations for government policy. On the one hand it does not pose so serious a threat for market structure, since the combine's share of any one market is less likely to be enhanced than in the case of a merger of two former competitors;[68] indeed the victim may be better able to challenge existing dominant firms in its own industry as a result of the takeover. On the other hand, where there are few overlapping activities the scope for some forms of economy will be limited; and the scope for an acquirer to apply superior expertise to raising the victim's profitability will be limited where this expertise is specific to the technology or markets of the acquirer's industry. And consequently, in terms of the determinants of profitability discussed in chapter 3, there will typically be fewer gains to be had by diversified merger from increased market power, and fewer by increased efficiency.

---

66 McClelland (1972), p. 29.
67 This presumes that the disciplinary role accorded by some to takeovers is denied by the evidence. See the discussion of this issue above.
68 The impact of a merger upon market structure has been a dominating concern of monopoly and merger policy. The criteria for referring mergers to the Monopolies Commission under the 1965 Monopoly and Mergers Act were that the merger would produce or enhance a monopoly, or that the victim exceeded a certain size. The direct impact of merger upon productive efficiency (less readily measurable or verifiable of course) has generally been considered only as a mitigating factor when dealing with actual references. Of course, the presumption has until recently been that efficiency gains would generally be available and realised (see chapter 3 above).

Table 3.F   The characteristics of mergers related to the degree of diversification

a. The average size of victims and acquirers as a percentage of the average for the Department of Trade and Industry quoted company population.

	Same 3 digit		Other 3 digit		Other 2 digit	
	Victim	Acquirer	Victim	Acquirer	Victim	Acquirer
Year	%	%	%	%	%	%
1964	13	141	16	143	56	191
1965	33	386	7	82	59	407
1966	107	375	11	109	27	487
1967	44	214	30	275	8	107
1968	38	99	120	431	37	245
1969	31	76	61	237	51	332
1970	27	256	15	710	33	127
1971	13	30	15	360	27	346
1972	21	37	9	78	42	746

Note: net assets is used as the size measure.

b. Victim's net assets as a percentage of joint net assets in the year preceding take-over.

All cases	30		23		20	
Number of cases	102		30		81	

c. The pre-merger profitability of victims and acquirers as a percentage of the profitability of the company's industry in aggregate for that year.

$y-3$	97.4	107.4	121.2	122.7	104.4	130.4[a]
	(35.9)	(48.1)	(52.5)	(47.1)	(50.1)	(44.0)
$y-2$	98.3	115.9[a]	115.4	122.9	107.0	137.0[a]
	(39.8)	(51.0)	(48.7)	(49.2)	(76.0)	(37.0)
$y-1$	89.6	120.6[a]	112.3	126.7[a]	99.9	131.1[a]
	(47.2)	(34.2)	(72.6)	(28.0)	(89.7)	(75.2)

Notes:
[a]   Significantly different from 100% at the 1% level.
y Year of merger.
The standard deviation appears in brackets beneath the mean.
Average profitability for the three years pooled:

3 years	95.1	114.6	116.3	124.1	103.8	133.5

See appendix C for the weighted average of both participants' profitability in the years before merger.

The definition of a diversified merger is not free of problems. The expedient adopted here has been to use the Department of Industry's (D.I.) allocation of companies to Standard Industrial Classifications, and to call diversified the acquisition of a victim in one classification by an acquirer in another. Of course, the D.I. can only allocate a company to a classification on the basis of the majority of the firm's activities; and often one or both of the merger participants will already be diversified, with both of them sometimes active in the same industry.[69] How-

69 See the evidence for 1951 on diversification in National Institute of Economic and Social Research (1956); and some suggestive evidence that diversification has since proceeded apace in Meeks and Whittington (1975b).

ever, no better information was available on which to classify the mergers; and so three groups were formed, comprising mergers within the same 3 digit industry (102 of the 213 cases studied in chapter 3), those in the same 2 digit, but a different 3 digit industry (30), and those in other 2 digit industries (81).

The hypotheses developed above (chapter 3) are again used; and the results are presented in a very similar form to those given in chapter 3. The change in profitability is reported using both the unadjusted and the adjusted measures described above, on the grounds that, while the adjusted measure is considered preferable, the adjustment procedure is unconventional, and parallel comparisons using the more usual (unadjusted) measure would act as a control on the conclusions, suggesting any oddities in the adjustment procedure.

The pre-merger characteristics of victims and acquirers

Table 3.F details certain characteristics of victims and acquirers in each of the three groups as did chapter 3 for all cases. Again the participants' size is expressed as a percentage of the average for the population in the same year.[70] For each of the three groups, as for the whole set of mergers, the acquirer is always bigger on average than the victim; and again, the average victim is in almost every year smaller than the population average, and the acquirer bigger. A comparison of the results for the three groups also suggests a weak tendency for the diversified acquirers to be biggest of the three groups on average.[71] Moreover, as section b. of the Table shows, the ratio of victim's to acquirer's size is smallest for the 'other 2 digit' group and largest for the 'same 3 digit' group.[72]

The participants' profitability record is detailed in section c. of the Table, and two conclusions reached for the whole set of mergers apply to each of the three individual groups. Firstly, the acquirer was typically more profitable than the victim prior to merger; and secondly, the acquirer was on average more profitable than the average for its industry-year. Again the victim was not greatly different from average in its profitability performance[73] (in none of the three pre-merger years, and in none of the three groups was the recorded difference from the industry reference level significant at the 1% level); although the 'same 3 digit' group performed rather less well and the 'other 3 digit' group better than average. Somewhat clearer distinctions emerged between the acquirers' records for the three groups: the 'other 2 digit' group clearly outpaced their industry, with profitability around a third higher than the industry (and levels significantly different from the 100% yardstick at the 1% level in all three years); while the 'same 3 digit' acquirer typically performed least well prior to merger.

---

70 The population (rather than industry) average provides a common yardstick when victim and acquirer belong to different industries: the size of the victim relative to that of the acquirer is not then obscured by differences in the industry averages of size.

71 Such a tendency would be the analogue of the tendency of larger companies to undertake more direct investment overseas – i.e. to diversify in terms of country – documented by Rowthorn (1971) p. 66.

72 See below for discussion of this association.

73 Though the 'other 3 digit' victims' average profitability was some 16% above average. However, individual observations were widely dispersed about the average, and the averages did not survive the significance tests used here as a control when interpreting the strength of differences.

Table 3.G The change in profitability after diversified and non-diversified merger: unadjusted profitability

	Same 3 digit				Other 3 digit				Other 2 digit			
	E	S_e	P	n	E	S_e	P	n	E	S_e	P	n
y	0.161[a]	0.102	0.333[c]	102	0.013	0.146	0.433	30	0.092[a]	0.090	0.395	81
$y+1$	−0.053[a]	0.168	0.576	92	−0.110[b]	0.269	0.654	26	−0.035[b]	0.139	0.554	74
$y+2$	−0.027	0.221	0.549	82	−0.147[a]	0.191	0.680	25	−0.002	0.147	0.493	67
$y+3$	−0.083[a]	0.189	0.594	64	−0.277[a]	0.429	0.727[c]	22	0.022	0.201	0.417	60
$y+4$	−0.037	0.205	0.646[c]	48	−0.337[a]	0.168	0.846[c]	13	−0.096[b]	0.283	0.643	42
$y+5$	−0.118[b]	0.260	0.563	32	−0.374[a]	0.080	0.875[c]	8	−0.021	0.198	0.630	27
$y+6$	−0.156[b]	0.282	0.545	22					−0.036	0.121	0.571	21
$y+7$	0.021	0.212	0.500	10					−0.216	0.430	0.800	10

Notes:
[a] Significantly different from 0 at the 1% level.
[b] Significantly different from 0 at the 5% level.
[c] Significantly different from 0.5 at the 5% level.

Full definitions are given in Table 3.B. E is the average change in profitability, and S_e its standard deviation; P is the proportion of companies for whom $E < 0$; n is the number of cases contributing to the average; y is the year of merger.

The average values of R for the various sets of amalgamations for each year are reported in appendix C.

Only one 'other 3 digit industry' amalgamation survived after $y + 5$; so no averages are reported thereafter for this group.

Table 3.H The change in profitability after diversified and non-diversified merger: adjusted profitability

	Same 3 digit				Other 3 digit				Other 2 digit			
	H	S_h	P	n	H	S_h	P	n	H	S_h	P	n
y	0.200[a]	0.109	0.284[c]	102	0.068[b]	0.135	0.400	30	0.112[a]	0.089	0.383[c]	81
$y+1$	−0.009	0.175	0.500	92	−0.043	0.255	0.615	26	−0.012	0.144	0.554	74
$y+2$	−0.005	0.233	0.524	82	−0.099[a]	0.158	0.600	25	0.017	0.156	0.478	67
$y+3$	−0.069[a]	0.194	0.594	64	−0.265[a]	0.428	0.636	22	0.030	0.199	0.417	60
$y+4$	−0.044	0.200	0.646	48	−0.329[a]	0.177	0.846[c]	13	−0.080[b]	0.282	0.619	42
$y+5$	−0.122[b]	0.257	0.594	32	−0.369[a]	0.082	0.875[c]	8	−0.018	0.199	0.630	27
$y+6$	−0.157[b]	0.280	0.545	22					−0.033	0.122	0.524	21
$y+7$	0.021	0.213	0.500	10					−0.217	0.431	0.800	10

Notes:
The notes to Tables 3.B. and 3.G. all apply here too; but in addition H is the counterpart of E when adjusted profitability (F) is used in place of raw profitability (R). The actual values of F are also given in appendix C.

Post-merger performance

The change in profitability after merger for the three groups is presented in Table 3.G (unadjusted basis) and Table 3.H (adjusted basis). In fact, all three sub-groups follow roughly the pattern described for the whole set in chapter 3 and no clear relationship emerges between post-merger performance and the degree of diversification. The worst record is that of the middling group, 'other 3 digit', which achieved both the smallest improvement in the year of merger (see chapter 3 on the unreliability of results for this particular year) and reported the worst decline in each subsequent year reported (significantly different from zero at the 1% level in four of the five years reported for both unadjusted and adjusted profitability).

The comparison of the polar groups, 'same 3 digit' and 'other 2 digit' does not reveal strong differences in post-merger performance. This runs counter to the expectation (justified above) that the non-diversified merger would typically offer the best hope of improvements in profitability. Such weak differences as do emerge suggest rather that the diversified group performs the better of the two, recording improvements in adjusted profitability in two years apart from the merger year, while in only one year is a decline significantly different from zero (and then only at the 5% and not at the 1% level); whereas in every year but y and $y + 7$ the non-diversified group records declines in profitability; and in three years the declines attain statistical significance.

Post-merger performance and the relative scale of victim and acquirer

Introduction

A central proposition in the work of Penrose and Marris[74] has been that beyond a certain point increases in a company's growth rate will exact costs in terms of productive or administrative efficiency. These costs are reckoned to stem chiefly from the difficulties of assimilating additions to the management team. They are incurred in expansion by new investment and by takeover alike, it is argued.[75] This section examines the proposition with respect to growth by take-over, comparing the post-merger performance of different quartiles of amalgamations distinguished by the proportionate contribution of the victim to the amalgamation's net assets. On the basis of the managerial theorists' arguments one might expect a merger which represented very great proportionate growth for the acquirer to prompt greater problems and less favourable subsequent profitability performance than one which represented only slight proportionate growth.

In addition there exists a mechanical relation between the victim/amalgamation size ratio and the impact of merger on the amalgamation's profitability, if it is assumed that any change in profitability is either confined or positively related to the victim's assets. If it is confined to the victim's assets, then say a one percentage point decline in the return on the victim's assets will correspond to a 1/3 point decline for the amalgamation if the victim is half the size of the acquirer, but to only a 1/11 point decline if the victim is a tenth of the acquirer's size.

74 See Penrose (1959), p. 212, Marris (1964), p. 114–18.
75 See Marris (1964), p. 123.

Table 3.I   The characteristics of mergers related to the relative size of victim and acquirer

a. The average size of victims and acquirers as a percentage of the average for the Department of Trade and Industry quoted company population.

	Quartile A		Quartile B		Quartile C		Quartile D	
	Victim	Acquirer	Victim	Acquirer	Victim	Acquirer	Victim	Acquirer
Year	%	%	%	%	%	%	%	%
1964	53	45	18	40	24	140	13	424
1965	23	23	58	173	47	319	36	662
1966	53	60	173	224	17	124	37	890
1967	33	38	19	61	68	292	14	539
1968	66	67	54	107	50	296	20	452
1969	80	48	32	77	45	214	63	1009
1970	41	28	30	61	19	172	12	805
1971	16	15	24	75	11	70	22	557
1972	41	17	7	22	15	124	33	589

Note: net assets is used as the size measure.

b. Victim's net assets as a percentage of joint net assets in the year preceding take-over.

	Quartile			
	A	B	C	D
All cases: mean	52	28	14	4
All cases: range	38–87	21–38	9–21	1–9
Number of cases	54	53	53	53

c. The relationship between diversification and the relative size of victim and acquirer (percentage of column total).

	Quartile			
Industry	A	B	C	D
Same 3 digit	64.8	54.7	39.6	32.1
Other 3 digit	11.1	18.9	15.1	11.3
Other 2 digit	24.1	26.4	45.3	56.6

$$X = \frac{D_{vy-1}}{D_{by-1} + D_{vy-1}} \quad \text{(see chapter 3 above)}.$$

Quartile A = top quartile by X
Quartile B = second quartile by X
Quartile C = third quartile by X
Quartile D = fourth quartile by X

The pre-merger characteristics of victims and acquirers

Section a. of Table 3.I reports the average size of the merger participants as a percentage of the population average for each of the four groups. The chief dissimilarities between the four groups are in the acquirer's size: typically, the smaller is X (the victim: amalgamation size ratio) the bigger is the acquirer. The

Table 3.J   The characteristics of mergers related to the relative size of victim and acquirer (continued)

The pre-merger profitability of victims and acquirers as a percentage of the profit-ability of the company's industry in aggregate for that year.

Year	Quartile A		Quartile B		Quartile C		Quartile D	
	Victim	Acquirer	Victim	Acquirer	Victim	Acquirer	Victim	Acquirer
$y-3$	85.4[a]	133.7[a]	102.1	114.7	99.7	118.4[a]	126.9[a]	106.2
	(24.1)	(64.7)	(41.2)	(52.5)	(41.3)	(33.3)	(62.4)	(36.4)
$y-2$	86.0[a]	143.8[a]	104.3	117.7	86.9	128.8[a]	139.3[a]	109.2
	(24.2)	(53.6)	(29.0)	(57.4)	(81.9)	(41.4)	(68.2)	(26.9)
$y-1$	80.4[a]	152.3[a]	94.5	124.3[a]	88.2	120.2	124.2	107.7
	(24.9)	(75.9)	(36.7)	(33.4)	(52.2)	(55.2)	(147.1)	(22.2)

Notes:
[a] Significantly different from 100% at the 1% level.
y Year of merger.
The standard deviation appears in brackets beneath the mean.
Average profitability for the three years pooled:

3	83.9	143.3	100.3	118.9	91.6	122.5	130.1	107.7
years								

See appendix C for the weighted average of both participants' profitability in the years before merger.

differences in victim's size follow no such regular pattern, however: in only two of the nine years does the ranking by victim's size follow that by X, whereas in six of the nine years the ranking by X is the exact reverse of that by the acquirer's size. Two other features of these subsets emerge from sections a. and b. of the Table. Firstly, the takeovers in quartile A are often 'reverse' takeovers: in many years the typical acquirer is smaller than the typical victim, and on average the victim sub-scribes more than half of the amalgamation's net assets. Secondly, the acquirers in quartile D are typically enormous (roughly 5 to 10 times the population average and 10 to 100 times the victim average), while those in quartile A (and often those in quartile B too) are relatively small (in all years below the population average).

Section c. of Table 3.I reinforces a suggestion made above. It shows the pro-portion of amalgamations in each quartile by X which belonged to each of the diversification categories used above. A majority of mergers in quartile A (high ratio of victim size to acquirer size) took place within the same 3 digit industry; while a majority of the takeovers which represented only slight proportionate growth for the acquirer crossed the 2 digit industry barrier.

On the profitability side reported in Table 3.J the middle quartiles, B and C, conform fairly closely to the pattern revealed for all classes in chapter 3 above. The two extreme groups, A and D, display some rather interesting differences from the average, however. On the one hand, for quartile A, where the victim was very large in relation to the acquirer, the participants have some of the features one would expect of a 'rescue' or disciplinary takeover: the acquirer's profitability is very high (significantly greater than the industry average at the 1% level in all three years, and more than 40% higher than the three-year industry average) and rising; whereas the victim's profitability is nearly 20% below the industry average (again the differ-

Table 3.K   The change in profitability after merger: quartiles by size of victim in relation to acquirer: unadjusted profitability

Year	Quartile A				Quartile B			
	E	S_e	P	n	E	S_e	P	n
y	0.283[a]	0.148	0.204[c]	54	0.098[a]	0.122	0.340[c]	53
$y+1$	−0.114[a]	0.119	0.681[c]	47	−0.039	0.342	0.563	48
$y+2$	−0.028	0.185	0.610	41	−0.024	0.352	0.535	43
$y+3$	−0.091	0.345	0.618	34	−0.152[a]	0.312	0.563	32
$y+4$	−0.077	0.411	0.609	23	−0.182[a]	0.211	0.762[c]	21
$y+5$	−0.056	0.352	0.538	13	−0.218[a]	0.217	0.615	13
$y+6$	−0.121[a]	0.077	0.625	8	−0.258[a]	0.125	0.714	7
$y+7$	−0.245[b]	0.168	0.800	5	−0.212	0.432	0.667	3

Year	Quartile C				Quartile D			
	E	S_e	P	n	E	S_e	P	n
y	0.059[a]	0.063	0.396	53	0.013	0.050	0.547	53
$y+1$	−0.031	0.137	0.500	50	−0.032[a]	0.082	0.574	47
$y+2$	0.020	0.121	0.438	48	−0.114[a]	0.106	0.619	42
$y+3$	−0.013	0.230	0.477	44	−0.042[a]	0.081	0.528	36
$y+4$	−0.022	0.290	0.630	27	−0.125[a]	0.097	0.688[c]	32
$y+5$	−0.016	0.178	0.529	17	−0.146[a]	0.194	0.750[c]	24
$y+6$	0.181[b]	0.208	0.273	11	−0.124	0.338	0.611	18
$y+7$	0.037	0.364	0.333	6	0.016	0.438	0.714	7

Notes:
[a]   Significantly different from 0 at the 1% level.
[b]   Significantly different from 0 at the 5% level.
[c]   Significantly different from 0.5 at the 5% level.

Full definitions are given in Table 3.B. E is the average change in profitability, and S_e its standard deviation; P is the proportion of companies for whom $E < 0$; n is the number of cases contributing to the average; y is the year of merger.

The average values of R for the various sets of amalgamations for each year are reported in appendix C.

ence survives the significance tests in all years), with some tendency to decline. On the other hand, in the case of quartile D, where a typically very large acquirer takes over a small victim, the pattern established by all the amalgamations studied (see chapter 3) is reversed: the acquirer's profitability is little different from the average for its industry-year, while the victim can boast clear superiority over its industry-year (a margin of some 30%, and one which is statistically significant at the 1% level in 2 of the 3 years). In other words, according to the criteria used here, a large mediocre company acquires a small successful one, often from another industry.

Post-merger performance

If attention is confined to the middle quartiles, B and C, then the records reported in Tables 3.K (unadjusted) and 3.L (adjusted) conform with the expectation outlined above. The quartile for which the takeover represented greater proportionate growth displayed the worst post-merger performance. In five of the post-merger years, quartile B experienced typical declines in adjusted profitability

Table 3.L The change in profitability after merger: quartiles by size of victim in relation to acquirer: adjusted profitability

Year	Quartile A				Quartile B			
	H	S_h	P	n	H	S_h	P	n
y	0.339[a]	0.143	0.167[c]	54	0.140[a]	0.122	0.302	53
$y+1$	−0.046[b]	0.139	0.574	47	0	0.331	0.542	48
$y+2$	0.016	0.222	0.561	41	−0.005	0.323	0.512	43
$y+3$	−0.062	0.357	0.588	34	−0.153[a]	0.306	0.594	32
$y+4$	−0.078	0.411	0.609	23	−0.183[a]	0.206	0.762[c]	21
$y+5$	−0.057	0.353	0.538	13	−0.214[a]	0.213	0.615	13
$y+6$	−0.123[a]	0.078	0.625	8	−0.253[a]	0.117	0.714	7
$y+7$	−0.246[b]	0.168	0.800	5	−0.212	0.432	0.667	3

Year	Quartile C				Quartile D			
	H	S_h	P	n	H	S_h	P	n
y	0.081[a]	0.061	0.358	53	0.028[a]	0.048	0.528	53
$y+1$	−0.003	0.142	0.480	50	−0.011	0.084	0.553	47
$y+2$	0.038	0.124	0.396	48	−0.095[a]	0.110	0.619	42
$y+3$	−0.007	0.229	0.455	44	−0.032[b]	0.080	0.500	36
$y+4$	−0.029	0.286	0.630	27	−0.116[a]	0.097	0.656	32
$y+5$	−0.025	0.179	0.588	17	−0.141[a]	0.197	0.750[c]	24
$y+6$	0.179[b]	0.211	0.273	11	−0.120	0.340	0.556	18
$y+7$	0.037	0.364	0.333	6	0.015	0.440	0.714	7

Notes:
The notes to Table 3.B. all apply here too; but in addition H is the counterpart of E when adjusted profitability (F) is used in place of raw profitability (R). The actual values of F are also given in appendix C.

(Table 3.L) greater than 15%; and in four of these years the declines were significantly different from 0 at the 1% level. Quartile C's declines on the other hand exceeded 4% in only 1 year; and only that year's decline was significantly different from 0 at the 5% level (not at the 1% level).[76] Moreover, for quartile C the number of companies reporting a decline in profitability represented a majority in only two of the eight years considered, whereas for quartile B a majority experienced a decline in all but the merger year.

It was argued above that the amalgamations in quartile A might be expected to suffer far sharper declines in profitability than those at the opposite pole, in quartile D, for two reasons. Firstly, the managerial theorists provide a convincing account of why moderate growth rates should produce relatively high profitability while very high rates of growth might beget difficulties for the maintenance of a creditable profitability record. Secondly, if it is assumed that any assimilation problems and consequent declines in profit will be some positive function of the size of the victim, then a victim which contributes a considerable proportion of the amalga-

76 Improvements in profitability recorded for y, the year of merger, are positively related to X across all four quartiles. This is consistent with the view that these apparent improvements result from measurement error: the bigger the victim whose accounts distort the picture, the bigger the distortion in year y (see chapter 3 above).

mation's net assets will be expected to have a greater effect on the amalgamation's profitability than one which represents only a small fraction of the amalgamation's size.[77]

The comparative experience of quartiles A and D runs counter to this expectation, however. The takeovers in quartile A were characterised above as the acquisition by highly profitable companies of relatively unprofitable victims of similar size to themselves (often even bigger). Yet their performance after merger did not suggest that they were suffering from massive assimilation problems. Only years $y + 6$ and $y + 7$, to which very few amalgamations contributed, revealed a decline in profitability greater than 8%; of the preceding years, one shows an actual improvement in profitability (apart from the merger year, y), and in only one does the decline pass the statistical test of significance at the 5% level.

It was expected that the amalgamations in quartile D (described above as typically resulting from the purchase of small successful companies by large ones with mediocre profitability records) would be relatively unaffected by the takeover. But they experienced declines in profitability no less severe than those in quartile A. Indeed, in four post-merger years, the decline exceeded 9%. Also, as the distribution of H was generally a good deal narrower for quartile D than for quartile A, three of the declines were significantly greater than zero at the 1% level; and a further one passed this statistical test at the 5% level. Finally, the proportion experiencing declines in profitability was greater for quartile D than for quartile A in four of the eight years studied.[78]

Conclusions to both studies

The study of separate subsets of mergers in this chapter had two objectives. The first was to see whether identifiable sub-groups of mergers displayed very different post-merger performance from the overall average reported in chapter 3. The second was to provide evidence on the impact of diversification and of Penrose effects. On the first issue, all seven of the sub-groups considered provided confirmation of the average picture reported in chapter 3. In the majority of post-merger years the typical amalgamation in any sub-group experienced a decline in profitability from the pre-merger level, whether or not profitability was adjusted for the accounting bias. Although the disaggregations performed here have not been exhaustive, it does appear that the average decline in profitability reported in chapter 3 was general over most types of takeover, and not the result of steep declines in an identifiable subset coupled with unchanged performance elsewhere.

No strong support was obtained for the very simple versions of the two hypotheses being considered, that more diversified mergers would be less successful in profitability terms, and that greater proportionate growth by merger would result

77 A study by Kitching (1967: see appendix C) found a high incidence of failure among takeovers where the victim was very small in relation to the acquirer. However, even were, say, 10% profitability converted into a 10% rate of loss for the *victim's* assets after takeover, this would produce only a negligible effect on the amalgamation's profitability if the victim represented only 1% of the amalgamation.

78 The managerial theorists' argument, that beyond a point further growth will depress profitability, is, of course, conducted in terms of the overall growth rate, not just the growth by merger isolated here (see chapter 5). It is conceivable that growth by means other than merger is systematically related to the rate of growth by merger in such a way that the managerial theorists' proposition is after all borne out by these companies in the case of overall growth.

in greater declines in profitability. The worse performance records were displayed by the middling groups, those in allied but not widely diversified industries (other 3 digit), and those in the second quartile by X.

Perhaps the most interesting and promising conclusions emerge from incidental comparisons that were made – especially those between the pre-merger profitability of participants in a particular group, and the amalgamation's subsequent success. These comparisons are especially striking for the two sets of extreme groups (same 3 digit: other 2 digit; top quartile by X: bottom quartile by X). In each comparison, the group whose acquirers had the highest average profitability prior to merger achieved much less bad performance afterwards than had been expected of them (the diversified in the first study, and quartile A in the second). By contrast, the groups which, on *a priori* grounds, should have been best able to raise, or avert declines in, profitability (same industry; those involving small proportionate growth) displayed a poor[79] record: and in both cases the acquirer's pre-merger record was the worst of the subsets being considered.[80]

These features of the participants lend some support to a generalisation that an acquirer with a relatively successful pre-merger record will typically be less unsuccessful at subsequently improving or maintaining profitability after merger. Were this generalisation to be corroborated by subsequent work, then an implication for merger policy could be to add criteria of previous performance to those (market share and victim size) which have previously dominated decisions to refer prospective mergers to the Monopolies Commission.[81] A policy ill-disposed towards the acquisition of the strong by the weak might both inhibit the type of merger which more often results in efficiency losses and provide an incentive to increase efficiency for those companies intending to expand through merger.

79 It was poor only in the light of expectations. The actual decline was not greatly dissimilar in absolute terms from that of the polar group (other 2 digit, large proportionate growth) with which it was being contrasted on *a priori* grounds.
80 These results suggest that the acquirer's size is a further feature which might exert an independent influence on the amalgamation's subsequent performance (and which might usefully enter a more elaborate multivariate analysis of the impact of Penrose effects and diversification). In the proportionate growth study, acquirers in quartile A, which performed less badly than expected, were relatively small; in quartile D, whose results were particularly disappointing, they were relatively large. In the diversification study, although the other 2 digit group runs counter to this tendency, the other 3 digit group typically contained larger acquirers, and displayed worse performance, than the same 3 digit group.
81 Confirmation of such a tendency would also weaken the support for one account of the decline in profitability after merger. This invokes the facts that acquiring firms tend to enjoy above average profitability, and that above average profitability tends anyway to regress towards the mean (see Whittington (1971), chapter 4 on this latter observation). Only if the post-merger decline exceeded the typical regression towards the mean associated with economic factors unrelated to the merger, would any decline be attributed to the merger. On this account it might be expected that acquirers with profitability considerably above average would typically record steeper declines than those with profitability around the average: but this chapter suggests the reverse.

4

Financing merger

From one point of view, the results of the previous chapter might seem surprising. Even if managers were willing (and allowed by imperfect product markets) to do other than single-mindedly pursue profit, would one not expect the capital market to have inhibited the provision of finance for projects such as takeover, which, on the evidence of chapter 3, typically led to a reduction in the efficiency with which assets were used? *Were* the capital market perfectly competitive and endowed with perfect foresight – so that finance was allocated to the projects offering the best returns – then the market would surely not have financed the average takeover whose results proved so disappointing: the assets of the potential victim would best have been left under the control of the existing management.

But even if this 'ideal' control has not prevailed, the literature suggests that there might remain an alternative control over the allocation of funds to companies. This is the one summarised in Marris' 'finance limit curve' mentioned in the previous chapter. Put very crudely, this control mechanism allocates the funds for expansion according to firms' current profitability on existing assets, whereas, of course, the 'ideal' system would allocate on the basis of the future profitability of the new project. Paradoxically, this alternative mechanism is believed to operate very largely *because of* imperfections in the capital market, especially uncertainty, which inhibit the effective operation of the 'ideal' control. For two of the principal features of this alternative control reflect imperfections in the market: firstly, because of capital market imperfections, managers are reckoned to display a strong preference for expansion from internally-generated funds, choosing to bypass the scrutiny and discipline of the capital market; and, secondly, even if managers do resort to the capital market, it is suggested that imperfections will foster a strong positive relationship between *current* profitability and the amount of external finance which the firm and the market are willing to entertain.

Management's reluctance to use external finance has been attributed to various factors which would be absent from a perfect market.[1] First, new issues entail a number of costs which are escaped with retention finance. Perhaps the most obvious are the transactions costs incurred with new issues, such as underwriting and registration costs.[2] In addition, the information on past and expected perform-ance that normally has to be provided in connection with a new issue exceeds that

1 The detailed arguments in the ensuing account rely heavily on Baumol (1965).
2 However, if (in order to avoid transactions costs) managers choose to retain profit rather than to distribute it, then shareholders who have to sell shares in order to meet their current cash needs will themselves be faced with additional transactions costs (see Wood (1975), (1975), p. 42).

ordinarily required in annual reports; and, apart from the direct costs of assembling this information, there exists the possibility that its disclosure to competitors will damage the firm's commercial position. Furthermore, a management group accustomed to a good deal of autonomy could resent in itself the outside scrutiny associated with new issues of shares or loans — a stronger possibility still if the issue carried with it restrictive provisions. And a further cost associated with a new issue — one that is emphasised in Wood's (1975) account — is the reduction in the price of a company's shares which typically takes place when a large number of new shares is offered at a single time. The consequent capital loss would be unwelcome to existing shareholders, amongst whom managers will sometimes number.

At least three other drawbacks of external finance receive attention in the literature. The first concerns uncertainty: an issue has to be planned some months ahead and its proceeds, sensitive as they are to the buoyancy of share prices in a market notorious for its turbulence, may be very difficult to predict.[3] Second, for an internally financed investment project to go ahead it is sufficient that the management should have favourable expectations of its returns, whereas, by contrast, for an externally financed project it is also necessary that 'the market' should concur with these expectations. Finally, the tax system may be adding a disincentive to distribute profits as they are earned, any new finance needed then being raised by external means: a penal rate of tax has been levied on dividends at certain stages in the post-war period.[4] This catalogue, probably even yet not an exhaustive one, lends some support to the expectation summarised by Galbraith (1972) that 'to minimise dependence on the (capital) market is . . . a universal planning strategy'.

If only these arguments are considered, one might expect growth-oriented managers with no ownership interest in the firm to retain the whole of (disposable) profit and eschew external finance. Then, the growth rate of net assets would be identical with the post-tax rate of profit of the firm and the crude alternative finance control would be totally effective: current profit would be the *sine qua non* of expansion. In practice, of course, firms typically do pay dividends and do not universally shun the capital market. But, it has been argued in the literature, neither of these modifications undermines the finance control because both retentions and external finance will be positively associated with current profit.

There are two types of reason why a less profitable firm could not always readily achieve the same growth rate from retentions as a more profitable one simply by retaining a bigger proportion of its (smaller) profit. The first reason is merely arithmetic: a firm with 10% profitability retaining all its income would, of course, be able to grow less fast from retentions than one with a 20% profit rate but which retained only three-quarters. As for the second reason, since dividends have some advantages for shareholders over retentions,[5] a management with any concern for its market rating will be reluctant to reduce dividends very much below the level of

3 To take a recent example of this turbulence, the industrial share index fell by 26% between June and December 1973.
4 See Whittington (1974), Table 1.
5 For one thing, the capital market cannot necessarily be relied upon to match the growth of the firm's assets because of retentions with a corresponding increase in the firm's market valuation. For another, even if the market value rises, realising retentions by selling shares imposes some transactions costs.

comparable firms'. This will particularly be the case for firms with low profitability, since a high retention ratio combined with below average profitability implies a most unfavourable ratio of dividends to capital.[6] Thus the scope for firms to compensate systematically for differences in profitability with differences in their retention ratio is held to be limited.

The arguments which suggest that the finance control will still be binding on firms which, notwithstanding the discussion above, are willing to have recourse to the market, emphasise that the amount of external finance that managements will seek or be able to raise will, like retentions, be positively related to the rate of profit. In the case of loan finance,[7] if future profits are uncertain and subject to fluctuation, managers are likely to feel reluctant to commit a very great proportion of future income to regular fixed interest payments for fear that sufficient profit may not be available in future years to meet these commitments. On this argument, firms are likely to adhere to some maximum desirable ratio of interest payments to total earnings;[8] and, other things equal, the larger are earnings, the more fixed interest capital firms will be willing to raise. In practice, of course, there are new share issues too; but their use is also likely to be positively related to current profitability. In conditions of uncertainty, current and recent performance may be reckoned by the capital market to be, though imperfect, yet among the best guides to future earnings and hence to the attractiveness of new issues. This is the response to uncertainty emphasised by Keynes (1936):[9]

> 'It is reasonable ... to be guided to a considerable degree by the facts about which we feel somewhat confident, even though they may be less decisively relevant to the issue than other facts about which our knowledge is vague and scanty. For this reason the facts of the existing situation enter, in a sense disproportionately, into the formation of our long-term expectations; our usual practice being to take the existing situation and to project it into the future, modified only to the extent that we have more or less definite reasons for expecting a change.'

Evidence of the market's reacting in this conventional way and favouring of firms with high current profitability can be found in the positive association between profitability and the valuation ratio (market to book value of the firm).[10] Of course, other things equal, with a higher valuation ratio (prompted by a higher profit rate), a smaller increase in the number of shares is required to elicit a given quantity of new finance (i.e. the cash is raised on more favourable terms, and, hence, presumably is raised more willingly). Thus on these arguments, external finance is a means not of removing the constraints imposed by retention finance altogether, but only of scaling up the flow of retentions.

Taken together, these arguments from the literature suggest that a growth rate much above average will not normally be achieved without above average profitability. The suggestion is that the very imperfections (especially uncertainty) which prevent the 'ideal' allocative mechanism from functioning effectively, lead to an

---

6 See the evidence in Singh and Whittington (1968, p. 260) that companies with low profitability typically did not have a relatively high retention ratio.
7 See Kalecki (1937).
8 Income gearing.
9 *General Theory*, Papermac Edition, p. 148.
10 See Singh and Whittington (1968), p. 63.

Table 4.A   The percentage of companies in the top third of the ranking by rate of growth of net assets belonging to the high, middle and low thirds of the ranking by profitability

Third by profitability	1948—64	1964—71
High	54.1	48.1
Middle	32.2	33.5
Low	13.7	18.3

Note: The annual rates of growth and profit are as defined in Tables 2.B and 3.D respectively.

alternative form of control, channelling new funds to firms with 'better' records at managing their existing capital.[11] And indeed considerable evidence has been assembled in the literature which is consistent with such an allocative process: a strong positive association has been found in cross-section between profitability and the rate of growth of net assets. Of course, as chapter 3 argued, it is not certain that the observed association can be attributed simply to the finance mechanism described here, and that the influence of the reverse relationship, the effect of growth upon profitability, can be ignored. However, as chapter 3 suggested, the common presumption in earlier work — that the effect of profitability upon growth is more uniform between firms (reflecting their relationship with a common capital market) and is the dominant factor behind the observed cross-section association — seems justified.

An early discussion of this subject (Marris (1964)) cites a number of previous empirical studies in support of its generalisation that 'the "representative" firm grows at about its (post-tax) net rate of return, while a firm with double the average growth rate needs about one and a half times the average profit rate'. A subsequent study of a larger set of companies for the fifties by Singh and Whittington (1968) also found a strong positive association between growth and profitability,[12] while acknowledging appreciable variations between industries and time periods — a result confirmed for a much wider range of industries in the fifties by Whittington (1971). Table 4.A confirms this impression for two post-war periods, 1948—64 and 1964—71. Investigating whether high growth was sustained without high profitability, it shows the percentage of companies in the top third of the rank order by net asset growth rate which belonged to each third of the ranking by profitability. In each period around a half of the fast growing companies were in the top third by profitability, but only around a sixth in the bottom third. Though high profitability does not in practice appear as a strictly necessary condition for rapid growth, nonetheless the proposition that the lower the rate of profit, the greater are the financing obstacles to rapid growth, is certainly consistent with the evidence.

Does this proposition apply with equal force to investment in new fixed and

11 Under this alternative control, finance will only flow to the most productive new investment projects if current profitability is the result of efficiency rather than of market power (see the discussion in chapter 3) and if profitability is a feature that persists. On the latter topic, see Reddaway (1967) and Whittington (1971).

12 They found that profitability was 'explaining on average about 50% of the variation in growth rates. A one percentage point increase in a firm's post-tax profitability on equity assets could be expected to lead on an average to a 0.7 percentage point increase in its growth rate.'

Table 4.B   Sources of finance of the typical continuing quoted company, related to particular uses of finance, 1964–71

Rate of growth (% of opening net assets, per annum):			
by retentions		5.1	
by external finance		6.7	
together = of total net assets			11.8
by *acquisition of subsidiaries:*			
financed by:			
retentions		1.7	
external finance		4.3	
of which:			
issues of shares and loans (in exchange)	3.2		
taking on minority interests and long term liabilities of subsidiaries	1.1		
Total		6.0	
by net *investment in new fixed and working capital*			
financed by:			
retentions		3.4	
issues of shares and loans (for cash)		2.4	
Total		5.8	
of total net assets			11.8
Net new investment in fixed capital		4.4	
Replacement investment (identified with and financed by depreciation) in fixed capital		5.5	
Gross investment in fixed capital		9.9	
Number of companies		966	

Notes:

All variables are simple averages across all company-years.

All variables are expressed as a percentage of opening net assets before averaging.

The reported values correspond exactly to those for the components of growth reported in Table 2.B. for 1964–71.

For fuller definitions see appendix B.

working capital on the one hand and to growth by acquisition on the other? As the first step in a discussion of this issue, Table 4.B examines the average contribution[13] of different sources of finance to each of these two components of growth for those members of the quoted company population which survived from 1964 to 1971.[14]

13 A sources of funds statement of the type presented in Table 4.B was compiled for each member of the population and the mean value computed for each variable. This is the same procedure, for the same set of companies, as Table 2.B above.

14 The corresponding exercise could not be carried out for the earlier period, 1948–64, as it normally is elsewhere in this study, because new issues were not then analysed by the Department of Industry into those for cash and those in exchange for new subsidiaries.

The table shows at once a marked contrast in the degree of reliance on retentions for the two forms of growth. Retentions financed the major part of net investment in new fixed and working capital (3.4%, i.e. 59% of a total 5.8% p.a.); and if replacement investment (assumed here to correspond to depreciation)[15] is added back, the percentage contribution of internally generated finance is greater still (77% of the total). The situation is reversed in the case of growth by takeover, however, the majority of which was financed from external sources (4.3%, i.e. 72% of a total of 6.0% p.a.).

This table suggests then that any constraint exercised by retentions upon expansion may, on average, have been less severe when that expansion took the form of takeover. This possibility and, more generally, the effect of profitability on the variance of rates of expansion by each of the two routes are examined in Figure 4.A and in Tables 4.C and 4.D. The diagram and tables describe the sources of funds for groups of companies distinguished according to their uses of funds. The diagram presents the growth and profit rates for various groups of companies and the contribution of retention and external finance to these growth rates for the period 1964–71. The tables provide more detail on these sources of finance and also comparable figures (where available) for corresponding subsets of the population which survived from 1948 to1964. In each case the population is ranked according to some growth variable: in Table 4.C according to growth by gross investment in new fixed assets,[16] and in Table 4.D according to growth by merger. In the former case, the population is divided into thirds,[17] low,[18] middle and high growth companies, with the latter category further subdivided into the top hundred by this ranking procedure, intensive growth companies, and the rest, appreciable growth companies. A slightly different procedure is adopted for Table 4.D: those making no acquisitions join one group (zero);[19] and it is the rest that are divided equally, this time to form two groups, low and high, with the high group again divided into intensive (the top 100 by this variable) and appreciable (the rest).

In the case of growth by investment in new fixed assets (figure 4.A and Table 4.C), the positive association between profitability and growth emerges clearly: without exception, the greater the rate of growth by investment within each period, the higher the rate of profit. As one might expect from this, more rapid growth by investment was associated with a greater contribution from retention finance: in 1964–71, growth by retentions for the intensive group was more than three times that for the low group (and in the earlier period it was more than twice as much). In addition, with one exception, the more rapidly growing and profitable the group, the higher was the ratio of external to retention finance. Overall, then, the picture provided for the financing of companies relying heavily on investment accords with that for earlier studies which distinguished companies only according to their growth of assets in total.

15 But see the discussion in chapter 2 and in Meeks (1974) of difficulties in inferring this correspondence.
16 Gross rather than net investment is the criterion used because of the difficulty of identifying replacement investment (see above).
17 In 1948–64, the numbers in each group are not exactly equal, because of ties in the ranking.
18 In each case, a tiny number of companies recording negative growth by that variable joined the low group.
19 On the grounds that these may represent a qualitatively distinct group – those eschewing takeover. There is no significant comparable group which eschewed investment: see chapter 2.

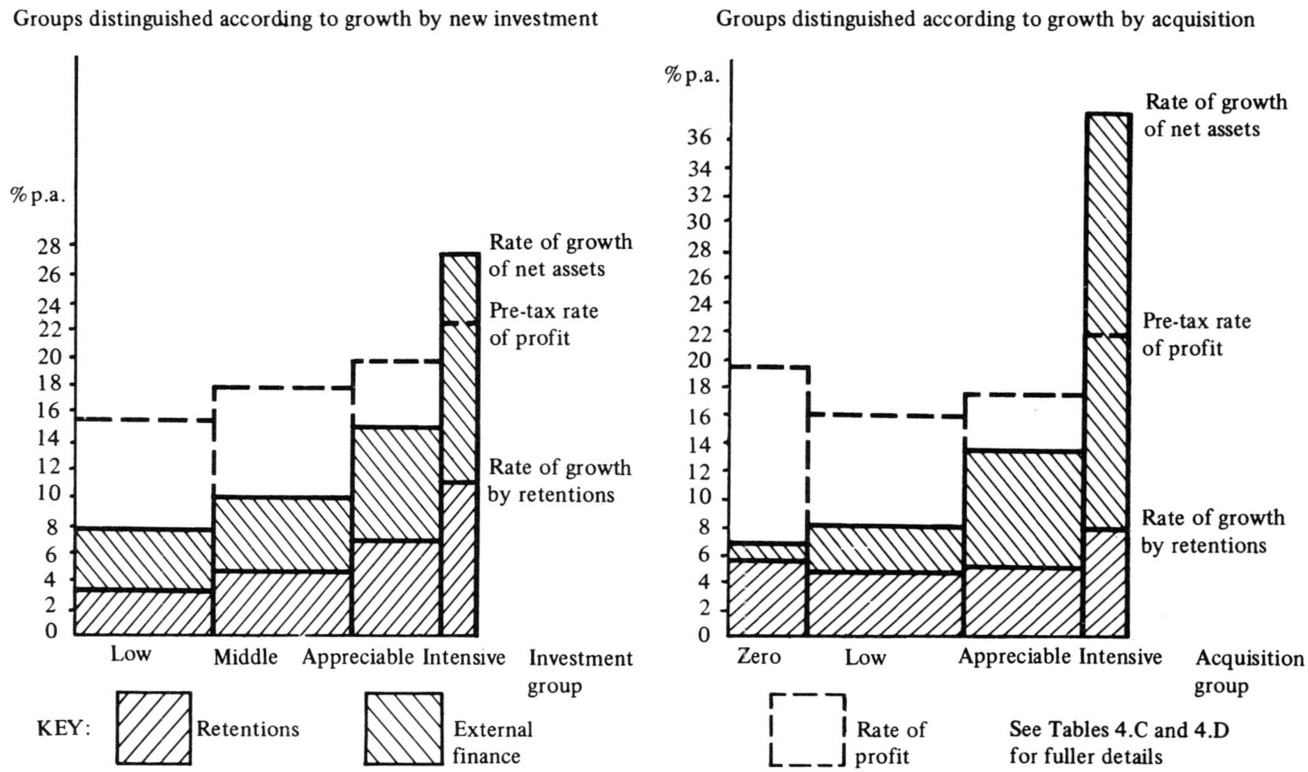

Figure 4.A. The financing of growth, 1964–71.

53

Table 4.C The financing of growth: sources of funds for subgroups of the ranking by gross new investment in fixed assets: continuing companies, 1948–64 and 1964–71

| | Category in the ranking by investment | | | | | | | | | |
| | 1948–64 | | | | | 1964–71 | | | | |
	Low	Middle	High	Appreciable	Intensive	Low	Middle	High	Appreciable	Intensive
Gross investment	3.0	6.6	12.9	10.6	20.0	4.0	8.5	17.3	13.4	26.0
Total sources of funds ≡ rate of growth of net assets	5.5	8.0	13.3	11.4	18.6	7.4	9.6	18.5	14.5	27.3
Rate of profit (pre-tax)	15.8	18.1	19.9	19.9	20.0	14.8	17.7	20.1	19.2	22.1
Growth financed by retentions	3.9	5.5	7.2	6.7	8.7	3.3	4.6	7.8	6.5	10.6
Growth financed externally:										
issues for cash						1.0	1.7	4.3	3.4	6.3
issues in exchange						2.1	2.3	5.2	3.5	8.9
minority interests, etc.						1.0	1.0	1.2	1.1	1.5
together	1.6	2.5	6.1	4.9	9.9	4.1	5.0	10.7	8.0	16.7
Ratio of external to internal finance %	41	46	85	70	114	124	109	123	137	158
Number of companies	415	417	418	317	101	322	322	322	222	100

Notes:
All variables represent the flow of funds for a year as a percentage of opening net assets, the values for each company-year being averaged for the group-period; the rate of profit is exceptional in that, following convention, *average* net assets are used as the denominator.
'Appreciable' and 'Intensive' are subgroups of 'High'.

For 'Appreciable' in 1948–64, individual sources of funds do not sum exactly to net asset growth because of rounding.

For fuller definitions see appendix B. For further accounting details of these groups of companies, see appendix D.

Table 4.D The financing of growth: sources of funds for subgroups of the ranking by expenditure on acquisition: continuing companies, 1948–64 and 1964–71

| | Category in the ranking by acquisition | | | | | | | | | |
| | 1948–64 | | | | | 1964–71 | | | | |
	Zero	Low	High	Appreciable	Intensive	Zero	Low	High	Appreciable	Intensive
Expenditure on acquisitions	0	0.1	4.9	2.7	14.3	0	0.3	11.7	5.9	28.6
Total sources of funds ≡ rate of growth of net assets	6.4	6.9	12.0	9.9	21.0	6.3	7.5	18.9	12.6	37.2
Rate of profit (pre-tax)	18.6	17.6	18.0	17.9	18.4	19.2	16.1	18.1	17.0	21.2
Growth financed by retentions	5.3	5.2	5.9	5.6	7.0	5.3	4.6	5.8	5.1	7.7
Growth financed externally:										
issues for cash						0.7	1.8	3.7	3.3	5.0
issues in exchange						0	0.2	7.7	2.9	21.6
minority interests, etc.						0.3	0.9	1.7	1.3	2.9
together	1.1	1.7	6.1	4.3	14.0	1.0	2.9	13.1	7.5	29.5
Ratio of external to internal finance (%)	21	33	103	77	200	19	63	226	147	383
Number of companies	202	524	524	424	100	188	388	390	290	100

Notes:
All variables represent the flow of funds for a year as a percentage of opening net assets, the values for each company-year being averaged for the group-period; the rate of profit is exceptional in that, following convention, *average* net assets are used as the denominator.

'Appreciable' and 'Intensive' are subgroups of 'High'.

For fuller definitions, see appendix B. For further accounting details of these groups of companies, see appendix D.

Table 4.E   The percentage of companies in the high group when ranked by growth by acquisition belonging to the high, middle and low thirds of the ranking by profitability

Third by profitability	1948–64	1964–71
High	32.1	35.6
Middle	35.9	35.4
low	32.1	29.0

Notes:
See appendix B for fuller definitions.

Table D.M. of appendix D provides comparable results for the high group by gross investment. The number of companies in the high group by acquisition is, of course, different from that in the high group by net asset growth (Table 4.A) or growth by gross investment (Table D.M.): see the definitions of these groups above.

In the case of growth by acquisition, however, any constraints which profitability might impose upon growth appear to have been much weaker. Figure 4.A and Table 4.D show that the ranking by profit rate fails to follow that by acquisition growth: in only one case (intensive in 1964–71) did a group which grew by acquisition enjoy profitability above the level achieved by those undertaking no acquisitions at all (and then only slightly greater) — though, *if* those making no acquisitions at all are set aside, a positive association appears between the two variables. Several groups did have a higher growth rate by retentions than the zero acquisition group, because the acquirers retained a bigger *proportion* of their profit; but these differences in the growth rate by retentions were too small to make more than a slight contribution to the differences achieved in the overall growth rate. When the intensive groups from each part of Figure 4.A are compared it emerges that the top 100 in the ranking by acquisition growth achieved an average overall growth rate some 10% p.a. higher than the top 100 by investment (and six times that of the scarcely less profitable zero acquisition group) despite a lower rate of profit and a rate of growth by retention some 3% p.a. lower. Of course, this was only possible because their reliance on external finance was much greater:[20] indeed both the high acquisition groups managed to scale up their retentions with external finance to a much greater extent than the groups growing rapidly by investment — even the appreciable acquirers group enjoyed a ratio of external finance to retentions (some 1.5) almost equal to that of the much more profitable group with intensive growth by investment. Extensive reliance on external finance was then a striking feature of the typical company growing rapidly by acquisition; and rapid growth by merger must often have been achieved without a specially creditable profit record[21] — a finding reinforced by Table 4.E. This is compiled on the same basis as Table 4.A, except that attention is focussed here on the high group according to rate of growth by acquisition, rather than by growth of total net assets as in the earlier exercise. And whereas in the case of net asset growth the high group was very well represented among the more profitable third of companies, and but weakly so in the low profitability group, here there is very little evidence of any

20 On the definitions used here, external finance plus retentions sum to net asset growth.
21 That the capital market has looked favourably upon acquiring companies is an inference which might also be drawn from the relatively high price-earnings ratios (other things considered) reported for them in the sixties (see the studies reviewed in appendix C).

systematic relationship. In the earlier period, just as large a proportion of the high acquisition group come from the low profitability group as from the high; and though in 1964–71 the high profitability group was very slightly better represented, the table does not suggest that low profitability constituted a specially severe obstacle to swift growth by means of takeover.[22, 23]

Yet if, as the results seem to show,[24] a finance control of the form suggested does operate fairly stringently in the case of new investment but only much more weakly for growth by acquisition, how is this to be reconciled with the *general* theoretical case presented earlier in this chapter? Perhaps the dissimilar treatment of the two forms of expansion might be rationalised to some extent by the fact that, with this particular finance control only operating at all because of uncertainty and other imperfections in the capital market, the degrees of uncertainty differ for the two forms of expansion; for there are two important respects in which uncertainty might be diminished when external finance is associated with takeover rather than with new investment. First, the company's uncertainty over the proceeds of an issue may be much smaller in a share for share (or loan for loan) exchange than in an issue for cash. The crucial variable in the case of share for share exchange is the exchange rate between the acquirer's and victim's shares: haphazard changes in the level of the market (which affect the proceeds of an issue for cash) will not affect the bidder's budgeting, provided that the relative position of the two shares remains the same. Second, the uncertainty attaching to the future earnings from the expansion may be smaller when it takes the form of takeover than when it consists of new investment. The problems associated with new investment – of

22 At first sight these conclusions might seem slightly at odds with findings of chapter 3 that the average acquirer was, at the time of acquisition, more profitable than its industry. It is of course the case that the intensive acquirers (who were well represented among the acquirers studied in chapter 3: see above) were somewhat more profitable than the other groups in 1964–71. What is being emphasised here is that a very minor profitability advantage over the rest is, for acquiring companies, associated with a very great growth advantage – greater than might have been expected had the growth taken the form of investment in new fixed assets.

23 One wonders whether these results for the whole population of companies pooled from all industries might owe something to a systematic influence of industry upon both profitability and the rate of growth by acquisition. Of course, the expectation, voiced in the earlier discussion of the identification problem arising over the association between profitability and growth, has been that, because of firms' relation with a common capital market, the finance relationship would dominate, not differing greatly among firms with diverse markets and technologies. And in fact the results reported in figure 4.B are consistent with this expectation: the picture appears to be qualitatively similar to that reported when all industries were pooled. The diagram reports the results of correlating, for the companies in each two-digit industry, the rate of profit with each of three growth variables: growth of net assets, growth by investment in new fixed assets (net) and growth by acquisition. The first section of the diagram, on net asset growth, confirms the positive association reported in earlier studies (see above): the correlation coefficients (one for each industry) cluster around 0.5. As the second section of the diagram shows, the distribution of correlation coefficients is similar when the correlation is performed instead for growth by net investment in new fixed assets: the values cluster around a slightly lower level, but none falls below 0.1. When the exercise is repeated for growth by acquisition, however, a different picture emerges (third section of figure 4.B), just as it did when the industry setting was ignored: the correlation coefficients cluster around a value much closer to zero. In a minority of cases, a negative correlation actually appears; and for only 2 out of the 18 industries does the coefficient exceed 0.3 (in contrast, it exceeded 0.3 for 14 industries in the case of total net asset growth).

24 And there are several qualifications which are discussed below.

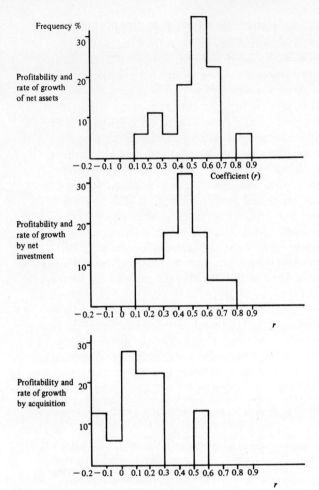

For individual coefficients, see appendix D, Table D.A.

Figure 4.B. Frequency distributions of industry correlation coefficients: profitability with various measures of growth: 1964—71.

using techniques of production and facing markets new to the management team —
may be less unpredictable in the case of takeover, a means of growth as a result of
which the *status quo* in the acquirer's and victim's factories and markets need often
be little altered. In the extreme case the acquirer might resemble a financial inter-
mediary, using its own equity to finance shareholdings in various firms, but not
intervening in the running of the subsidiaries. Growth by takeover would then
become akin to portfolio management, and the constraints on the growth of the
portfolio as a whole much weaker than those on the internal expansion of any individual enterprise within it.[25]

Of course, although these factors may help to explain *why* the finance control
was less stringent in the case of growth by takeover, they neither alter the fact that
it did indeed appear to operate relatively feebly nor diminish the significance of the
findings of chapter 3 that poor performance after merger accompanied this weak-
ness of the finance control mechanism.

Some caveats
A number of qualifications must be attached to the conclusions presented
in this chapter. First, it has been presumed, following the discussion in chapter 3,
that it is profitability's effect on growth — Marris' 'finance limit curve' — which has
been identified. The arguments for this presumption are strong, but not incontro-
vertible.

Second, the treatment of timing in this chapter is not altogether satisfactory:
average levels of profitability and rates of growth have been measured over a period
of several years, and this somewhat obscures the distinction between profitability
before and after the growth has occurred. A more sensitive specification of timing
aimed at separating these two phases might be worthwhile, although, as was seen in
chapter 3, it would present difficulties.[26]

Third, the exercises reported — for instance, the simple correlation of profitability with a single component of growth, such as takeover — probably imply too
simple a relationship. It seems plausible that the amount spent on takeover might
depend, on the financing side, not just on total income but also on appropriations
from income such as dividends and taxation, on other allocations of retained profit
such as investment in new fixed and working capital, and on the present liquidity
and future capital needs of both the acquirer and potential victims. This list is not,
of course, exhaustive; but clearly much more sophisticated analysis would be
possible, and so the results provided here are best regarded as preliminary and
suggestive.

Summary and conclusions
A traditional analysis would show that in a perfectly competitive capital

25 This does not rule out the possibility of efficiency losses. On the contrary, the fact that
little need change after merger undermines the chief justification for merger cited above —
that it will act as a catalyst for improvements in efficiency. All it might mean is that
merger provides a relatively low risk, low effort avenue to greater size with resulting benefits for management (see chapter 3).
26 Whittington's (1971 and 1972) work on the relationship between profitability and external
finance took this into account, and his current development of that work, making a
distinction between external finance for cash and for new subsidiaries, should bear on the
issues raised here.

market with perfect foresight finance would not have been available for mergers which promised a reduction in the efficiency with which assets were used. It has been argued in the literature that the capital market is imperfect, but that its very imperfections, perhaps particularly uncertainty, might contribute to an alternative crude control over the allocation of finance: given plausible assumptions about dividend payments and the rates at which internal finance will be matched with external, achieving a growth rate above average will be difficult without above average *current* profitability. Although such a control is consistent with the evidence in the case of growth by new investment, however, past experience suggests that it could only have operated feebly for growth by merger. Any reluctance to resort to external finance must have been much less strong for growth by merger: a major proportion of growth by acquisition (but not of new investment) was typically financed from external sources; and whereas a strong positive association was found between profitability and the rate of growth by new investment, that between profitability and the rate of growth by takeover was very much more weak.

This chapter certainly raises more issues than it settles, and, especially in view of the qualifications detailed above, demonstrates the need for more research on the role of the stock market in financing merger. But the ability of companies with mediocre profit performance to grow rapidly by takeover, coupled with the evidence of chapter 3 on the disappointing outcome of the typical merger, provokes considerable doubts about the effectiveness of market controls over acquisition and reinforces the case for tighter restrictions and additional appraisal by the state.

5
Other characteristics of acquiring companies

Size and growth by merger

Is growth by merger more readily undertaken by companies of above average size? Some advantages have been claimed in the literature for firms of large scale which, if they did indeed materialise, should enhance internal efficiency and presumably the ability to expand; but, as chapter 3 reported, the evidence to support these general claims is not impressive. There are, however, factors unconnected with the relative efficiency of large and small firms which could yield an advantage to the larger in pursuing growth by merger. First, it is well documented[1] that the unit costs of raising new issue finance decline with the size of the issue. Thus, since growth by takeover is typically so heavily financed from external sources (see chapter 4), the larger firm will be at an advantage in achieving a given rate of growth by merger. Second, technical factors may sometimes dictate, or it may simply chance, that there exist within an industry[2] no firms below a certain size suitable for acquisition; then, if assimilation problems mount as the ratio of victim's size to acquirer's size increases – as surely they must at some point[3] – the larger firm may be more willing to acquire one of the potential victims.

Some confirmation of this expectation is found in the evidence both of Singh (1971 and 1975) and of chapter 3 above, that acquiring firms were bigger than their victims and than their industry average. In addition, a study which compared the growth performance of giant companies and the rest of the population (Meeks and Whittington (1975b)) showed that these very big companies excelled the rest in their rate of growth by merger.[4]

However, whilst not contradicting these earlier findings, since the majority of those involved in merger appear to be bigger than average, Table 5.A does not

---

1 See, for example, Davis and Yeomans (1975).
2 Either the acquirer's industry or one into which it wishes to diversify.
3 Imagine the extreme case of the corner shop assimilating I.C.I. See the discussions of assimilation problems in chapter 2, and chapter 3 and its appendix, and the second half of this chapter.
4 If the proportionate contribution of growth by acquisition to overall net asset growth did not vary with the size of the firm, then the literature on size and overall growth would bear directly on the issue of this chapter. One recent contribution to this literature (Singh and Whittington (1975)) found a mildly positive relationship between size and growth for British companies in the period 1948–60. Another (Meeks and Whittington (1976)) suggested a nonlinear relationship: while the bigger companies grew faster than those of middling size, it was the smaller ones which grew fastest of all.

    However, it is not certain that the proportionate contribution of growth by merger does not vary systematically with firm size (see Meeks and Whittington (1975b)); and it may not be possible to generalise directly from these results to the relationship between size and growth by merger.

Table 5.A The average opening size of groups distinguished first, according to their rate of growth by acquisition and, second, according to their rate of growth by gross investment in fixed assets

	Net assets (£ million)					
Rate of growth by acquisition	Overall average	Zero	Low	High	Appreciable	Intensive
1948–64	2.55	0.75	2.94	2.86	3.31	1.03
n	1250	202	524	524	424	100
1964–71	12.26	5.18	15.20	12.74	14.74	6.94
n	966	188	388	390	290	100
Rate of growth by gross investment	Overall average	Low	Middle	High	Appreciable	Intensive
1948–64	2.55	2.14	2.90	2.61	2.67	2.42
n	1250	415	417	418	317	101
1964–71	12.26	12.74	13.65	10.39	12.34	6.04
n	966	322	322	322	222	100

Notes:

n is the number of companies contributing to the group average

'Appreciable' and 'Intensive' are subgroups of 'High'.

See appendix B for fuller definitions.

suggest that the relationship between size and growth by merger is a simple linear one. This Table records the average opening size of the various groups in the ranking according to growth by merger used earlier. In both periods the middling groups by growth by acquisition were typically bigger than average, whereas the two extreme groups of zero and of intensive acquisition were each typically much smaller than average. The differences are striking, the intensive group being less than half the average size of the appreciable group, and the zero group smaller still on average.[5] These results do certainly mean that large size, whatever its advantages for merger, is not a necessary condition of high rates of growth by acquisition; and they suggest too that some fluidity may be obtained in industrial structure, since some small companies seem able to use this means of growth to enhance their size and so eventually perhaps to challenge those currently dominating the economy. Table 5.A also reports the size of subgroups of the population segregated according to the rate of growth by gross investment in new fixed assets, for comparison with the results on growth by takeover. In fact the pattern which emerges is qualitatively similar to that for growth by takeover – in both periods the intensive growth companies were typically smaller than average, as was the average member of the low group in 1948–64 – but on the whole the differences are more muted. These results for the two components of growth are of course consistent with that earlier work[6] which has found that the dispersion of performance variables such as the growth rate and profitability declines with size: in view of this earlier evidence one

5 Though, given the skewness of the size distribution (see Singh and Whittington (1968)), allowance must be made for the possibility of a small number of very large companies having a disproportionate effect on the mean of a particular group.
6 E.g. Whittington (1971), Singh and Whittington (1975) and Meeks and Whittington (1975b).

would not have expected, despite the theoretical considerations, the larger companies to be so highly represented at the extremes of a distribution by rate of growth.

Thus, whilst, as earlier studies have suggested, large firms were generally active in expansion by merger (those achieving middling growth rates by merger being typically bigger than average), it could not be said that this form of growth was the exclusive preserve of big firms. Indeed, very rapid growth by merger was associated with initial size below average.

Growth by new investment and growth by merger

The conclusions arrived at in chapter 3, that growth by merger appears often to have been achieved at the expense of profitability, lends some support also to the argument that growth by merger may displace investment in new fixed assets; for the assimilation problems apparently associated with merger might pre-empt managerial resources which would otherwise be available to commission entirely new capacity. This would only be the case if there were some constraint upon the supply of managerial resources in total, since otherwise even a troublesome merger need not oust investment; but Penrose (1959) and some subsequent 'managerial' theorists of the firm have argued that the availability of management will indeed be limited since special difficulties are likely to beset firms which attempt to assimilate very great proportionate additions to their management team (see Chapter 3 and its appendix). Thus the need to limit such 'Penrose effects', which could depress profitability, would dictate a ceiling to the overall rate of expansion and consequently a trade-off between alternative means of growth.[7] Of course, it is not just because of assimilation problems that a trade-off might exist: expansion by merger might, for instance, reduce the finance available for new investment (see Chapter 4 on financial constraints). Again, a merger with a former rival might reduce the pressure to invest in capacity which promised lower cost or higher quality – though, as against this, a merger might eliminate one element of insecurity which was formerly inhibiting investment.[8]

In certain circumstances the trade-off facing the individual firm would be represented by the observed relationship for a cross-section of firms between the rate of growth by acquisition and that by new investment.[9] This would be the case if the same ability and willingness to grow characterised all firms, the feasible combinations of growth rates by takeover and by new investment being common to them all. Then all that would distinguish firms' expansion would be their choice between takeover and new investment as means of growth, and the scatter of

7 Even though it might be possible to achieve a *higher* growth rate by external than by internal means before falling foul of assimilation problems (see Chapter 2), on the Penrose argument this would mean not that the constraint was removed but only that the constraint on the overall growth rate was higher, the bigger the share of external in total growth.

8 These issues are discussed in George (1972).

9 In some circumstances, even if a negative association between investment and merger were observed it would not carry the implication that merger displaced investment. This would be the case when firms only undertook merger when there was little or no possibility of investing. Thus, over time the two variables might be inversely correlated because growth-oriented firms merged actively when investment prospects were dim (the analogue of the situation described by Rowthorn (1971) whereby firms in sluggish home economies seek expansion abroad). Or a cross-section counterpart of this might be that firms in industries facing stagnant or declining demand resorted to takeover in order to achieve expansion.

Table 5.B   The average rate of growth by new investment of groups distinguished according to their rate of growth by acquisition

| | Rate of growth by acquisition | | | | | |
	Overall average	Zero	Low	High	Appreciable	Intensive
1948—64						
Gross investment	7.5	6.3	6.9	8.6	7.8	11.8
Net investment	3.7	2.9	3.1	4.5	3.8	7.4
n	1250	202	524	524	424	100
1964—71						
Gross investment	9.9	7.9	9.2	11.6	10.6	14.6
Net investment	4.4	3.5	3.8	5.5	4.7	7.8
n	966	188	388	390	290	100

Notes:

n is the number of companies contributing to the group average.

'Appreciable' and 'Intensive' are subgroups of 'High'.

See appendix B for fuller definitions.

observations on the two variables for different firms would indeed represent the options facing the individual firm. In practice, such conditions of strict uniformity between firms are of course not likely to be fulfilled. As was argued in Chapters 3 and 4, in the discussion of the identification problem encountered when relating growth and profitability in cross-section, the rate of growth at which further expansion would impair efficiency is likely to differ a good deal between firms, and this would mean too that the combination of growth rates by the two means which was consistent with a given profitability target would vary from firm to firm. For not only external factors, such as the growth of markets and the flow of technical progress, but also the diversity of management ability are likely to cause differences in this critical rate of overall growth.[10] Thus firms in a favourable environment and/or with more capable management than average may have been able to achieve more rapid rates of growth by both internal and external means than their less favoured or proficient counterparts; and yet it could still be true that these firms might have been willing and able to invest in new assets more heavily if fewer of their senior management resources had been devoted to assimilating new subsidiaries.

However, even though differences in firms' willingness and capacity to grow are likely to have obscured any underlying trade-off between takeover and new investment, it still seemed worthwhile reporting the observed relationship between the two variables in cross-section, partly to show whether a negative association emerged despite inter-firm differences and partly to detail one further feature of acquiring companies which has not been described in earlier chapters. Accordingly, Table 5.B reports some features of the observed cross-section association between the two variables for continuing members of the quoted company population for the two post-war periods. The table shows that, universally (and whether a gross or

10 See the appendix to Chapter 3 on the lack of a systematic association between the post-merger profitability decline and the proportionate growth represented by the merger.

Table 5.C   The regression of growth by new investment upon growth by takeover, 1964—71

$I = a + b.A + e$, where I = rate of growth by gross investment, A = rate of growth by acquisition and e = error term.

Industry		a	S_a	b	S_b	R^2	n
21	Food	13.70	1.18	−0.43[*]	0.11	0.35	30
23	Drink	5.89	0.46	0.20[*]	0.09	0.10	49
26	Chemicals, etc.	10.10	0.95	0.28[*]	0.09	0.19	49
31	Metal manufacture	9.55	0.97	0.07	0.15	0.01	43
33	Non-electrical engineering	6.70	0.43	0.30[*]	0.07	0.15	117
36	Electrical engineering	9.01	1.16	0.17	0.13	0.03	54
38	Vehicles	8.68	1.42	0.42	0.22	0.11	31
39	Metal goods not elsewhere specified	7.22	0.66	0.27[*]	0.10	0.10	70
41	Textiles	8.81	0.75	0.10	0.12	0.01	71
44	Clothing and footwear	4.85	0.95	0.31[*]	0.11	0.20	33
46	Bricks, pottery, etc.	10.34	0.96	0.40[*]	0.09	0.32	40
47	Timber, furniture, etc.	8.43	1.39	0.66[*]	0.24	0.21	32
48	Paper, printing etc.	8.46	0.89	0.24	0.14	0.05	57
49	Other manufacturing	9.34	1.18	0.25	0.15	0.07	39
50	Construction	13.60	1.88	0.41[*]	0.20	0.07	57
81	Wholesale distribution	8.14	1.18	0.27	0.16	0.04	78
82	Retail distribution	6.63	1.46	0.83[*]	0.21	0.16	82
88	Miscellaneous services	11.90	1.62	0.13	0.17	0.01	49

Notes:
n is the number of companies within the industry; industries with only a very small number of observations were excluded from the exercise.

[*]means that the slope coefficient is significantly different from zero at the 5% level.

See appendix B for fuller definitions.

net investment measure is adopted), a more rapid rate of growth by acquisition in fact went hand in hand with a higher rate of growth by new investment. True, the differences between the zero, low and appreciable acquisition groups were not large, but the intensive acquirers achieved an investment rate much above average. Moreover, the positive association between the two variables survives when the data are stratified by industry: Table 5.C shows the results of regressing the rate of growth by investment upon that by acquisition for the companies in each 2 digit industry.[11] For seventeen of the eighteen industries reported the slope coefficient in the regression is positive and in nine cases significantly greater than zero at the 5% level.

The active acquirer appears then to have invested more heavily than average in new fixed assets too. Some reasons were given above why these observations might yet be consistent with individual firms facing a trade-off between the two forms of growth. But a different form of analysis would be necessary before the opponent of the state's tolerance of merger could maintain in his catalogue of merger's costs the empirical generalisation that it inhibits new investment.[12]

11 Four of the twenty-two industries available, each with very few member companies, were excluded from the exercise.
12 It has been implicitly assumed in this discussion that new investment is socially desirable on the grounds that it commonly brings new products, the embodiment of technical progress, increased output per man, etc.

6

Implications for state policy

It was shown in chapter 2 how prominent growth by merger has been in recent years; and the chapters that followed it have yielded three generalisations with particular relevance to state policy on merger. Firstly, there appear to be financial (and other) incentives to managers who have little or no ownership interest in the company to pursue growth even at the expense of profitability (chapter 3). Second, the efficiency gains, which in public policy statements have been assumed to be the saving grace of growth by takeover, cannot in the event be relied upon: strong evidence was reported that the efficiency of the typical amalgamation did not improve after merger (chapter 3) — it actually appears to have declined. Finally, the finance constraint which has been cited as strongly favouring more profitable companies seems to operate much more weakly for growth by takeover than for growth by new investment: much less reliance is placed on retention finance and many of those growing fairly rapidly by takeover, and gaining external finance to do so, were unremarkable for their profitability (chapter 4).

Any of these three generalisations alone might cause concern over the United Kingdom's permissive policy towards merger; but together they prompt alarm. In the light of this evidence, it would seem reasonable to reverse government policy, incorporating a presumption against takeover, with the onus put on merging companies to demonstrate that, in practice, non-trivial efficiency gains[1] can be expected to result from the merger:[2] if the proponents of unrestricted takeover activity disagree with these policy prescriptions, likewise the burden of proof is surely now thrown on them. At the very least such a shift of attitude should prompt closer appraisal of merger by the participants: on the evidence of Newbould's (1970) study, weak appraisal might bear considerable responsibility for the disappointing performance of merged companies documented above.

If it is the case that acquirers with a more creditable pre-merger profitability record are more successful after merger too, a proposition gaining some incidental support from the appendix to chapter 3, then as part of any policy change there might well be a case for adding past performance to the criteria (size and market share) already used in screening mergers: more detailed scrutiny could perhaps be devoted to prospective mergers where the acquirer's profitability record is less good

1　Allowing for both productive efficiency — in the sense used above — and any changes in allocative efficiency.
2　A precedent for the state presuming that a practice was undesirable unless those involved could demonstrate otherwise is provided by the 1956 Restrictive Trade Practices Act.

than average or than the victim's.[3] Not only would such a step inhibit the acquisition of the relatively efficient by the inefficient, but also it would act as a ginger to those anxious to grow by takeover; and, unlike a blanket hostility towards merger, it would still allow small but dynamic companies to use this means of growth to challenge large entrenched ones (as existing arrangements do: see chapter 5). But a detailed assessment of alternative policies, and of the considerable difficulties presented by any of the options, is not attempted here:[4] the main aim is to argue for a change from the present presumption that efficiency gains will more often than not follow merger.

One other side effect of a more stringent policy towards merger might be to channel the evident growth aspirations of those currently growing by acquisition into the major alternative form of growth, new investment in fixed assets. It is difficult to demonstrate that, in the past, growth by acquisition has come at the expense of growth by new investment (see chapter 5). But the evidence of chapter 3 does suggest that mergers have often caused assimilation problems which must have absorbed some of the energies of company directors, energies which, had many of these takeovers been inhibited, could have been diverted to deal with additional new investment and the assimilation problems associated with that. Not only does this alternative form of growth carry strong possibilities of socially desirable consequences (increased labour productivity, challenge to existing market positions, new products, embodiment of technical progress, etc.), but also it appears (from chapter 4) to be more susceptible to the finance control which allocates the means of expansion to those with the better profitability records.

Marriage then having so often proved disappointing and divorce from merger being disruptive itself, why *not* encourage some celibacy now?[5]

---

3 True, a profitable firm may not necessarily be efficient (it may owe its performance to a strong monopoly position); but a persistently unprofitable company (compared with say the industry average) is surely unlikely to be specially efficient.

The inadequacies of historic cost accounting (see appendix B and Meeks (1974)) also present difficulties for such a policy. It may be hoped, however, that the current reappraisal of accounting under inflation will soon produce a less imperfect measure of profitability.

G. Whittington suggested one potential abuse of such a policy: where a bid was uncontested and the actual acquirer was the less profitable, the actual victim might purport to be the acquirer. More careful scrutiny would be required to close this loophole.

4 See Sutherland (1971 and 1975) and Utton (1975) for detailed discussion of alternative policies.

5 Not, however, excluding affairs. See Richardson (1972) on fruitful associations outside wedlock.

Appendix A. The valuation of acquired companies, and its impact on profitability

Introduction

In a regime of rising prices, the book value of companies' assets (which for the most part represents their historic cost) typically understates their realisable value. When a company is taken over, the acquirer often pays more than the book value of the victim, and sometimes enters the victim in its own books at a value exceeding that in the victim's books prior to the merger. This excess will normally be entered in the acquirer's balance sheet under the asset heading 'goodwill'; the victim's assets will then be added to the other components of the balance sheet at historic cost. In these cases of revaluation, the rate of return of the amalgamation (profit ÷ average book value of net assets) will be lower than the weighted average rate of return for the two separate entities would have been in the absence of merger, for a bigger denominator (incorporating goodwill) is used in calculating profitability.[1] Although accounting conventions prompt a clear expectation of a bias in any profitability results (one which would in fact weaken if not reverse the typical conclusions of earlier work) only Singh's study makes explicit allowance for it. He dismisses it, however, as slight, and insufficient to modify his results seriously. Nevertheless, inflation has continued apace since Singh's period of study (the late fifties), and it seems likely that premia over book value will have been increasing.

The available data on merger valuation and the estimation of goodwill arising on consolidation

Three values of a new subsidiary may be distinguished (although two or even all three may in some cases be identical):

$V.1$: the valuation attributed by the Department of Industry (D.I.) from 1964.

$V.2$: the amount at which the acquisition is recorded in the acquirer's balance sheet.

$V.3$: the value of the victim in its own balance sheet, prior to acquisition.

Before 1964, $V.1$, the D.I.'s valuation in the flow of funds statement was taken as $V.2$. It was defined as the 'cash paid plus the value of shares . . . issued by a company for a controlling interest . . . in another company. The value of shares is that

---

1 A further bias exists in the calculation of the rate of return for an amalgamation in the year of takeover, because of the problem of aggregating the victim's and acquirer's accounts in that year. This is discussed in chapter 3.

attributed to them in the accounts of the acquiring company.'[2] From 1964, however, the D.I. provided, wherever possible, a current valuation of the newly acquired subsidiary, defined as:

> '... the cash paid or the market price at the date of issue of shares or loan stock issued ... Where market values are not available [not generally the case for the quoted companies dealt with here] or the cash consideration is not disclosed [sometimes it would be difficult to infer this value from companies' accounts before the 1967 Companies' Act, which required more detailed disclosure of changes in assets and reserves] acquisitions are in general valued at the net book value of the acquired company.'[3]

However, there is no statutory requirement of companies that they disclose the market value of the shares and stocks which they issue in exchange for new subsidiaries (in fact, company reporting of acquisitions leaves much to be desired: often neither $V.1$ nor $V.2$ nor $V.3$ is detailed in companies' accounts – see Lee (1974)). The D.I. obtains this information from the Stock Exchange Weekly Intelligence and from the financial press. $V.1$ appears in the Data Bank at $T73$ (consideration for subsidiaries) from 1964; and this is the valuation used (along with information on trade investments, etc.) at $T39$ (expenditure on subsidiaries and trade investments) in the Uses of Funds Statement (see appendix B). Hence it is the measure used, from 1964, in the net assets growth measure employed elsewhere in the study.[4]

The D.I. have typically provided $V.3$ in the computer file of company accounts, but only since 1964. This information appears at $T78$ to $T87$ and $T90$ (composition of subsidiaries' assets) in the Data Bank, where the D.I. analyse the accounts of the victim prior to acquisition (this analysis of the subsidiary's net assets into its component asset headings also enables the D.I. to exclude from uses of funds headings, such as investment in fixed assets, the change in the balance sheet heading, fixed assets, due simply to the takeover, and not representing purchases of new fixed assets). However, the D.I. does not perform this analysis for all acquisitions: only an assumed total book value is provided where the purchase consideration ($V.1$) is less than £0.9 million or the victim is a foreign registered or private exempt company. Since the threshold is defined in terms of *market* value, however, victims with a *book* value of much less than £0.9 million are often analysed by the D.I. (*N.B.* mergers with quoted victims whose accounts have not been analysed by the D.I. are still included in the sample studied in chapter 3: these exclusions apply only to the valuation study reported below). Nevertheless, increases in asset headings in the uses of funds statement will be distorted when a company acquires another which does not fall within the categories for analysis: increases in assets will include the stocks of assets purchased with the new subsidiary, and, since the purchase price also appears as a use of funds at $T39$, a balancing adjustment appears

---

2 Central Statistical Office (1963).
3 Department of Industry (1975).
4 See especially chapter 4.
   $V.2$ represents the actual change in the acquirer's net assets; but it is arguable that $V.1$, being based on current values, is more consistent with other components of net asset growth, such as investment in new fixed assets which are measured in current values. Problems do arise in comparing $V.1$ between individual years, however: it is a volatile measure moving with the often violently fluctuating level of stock market prices.

under $T44$, the consolidation adjustment. This problem will often be trivial in the case of very big acquiring companies, but could be more serious for smaller ones.[5]

In the years since 1964, the period of the merger study, $V.2$ is not provided separately in the D.I.'s computer record, and hence not in the Data Bank either. Yet this is the critical value for assessing the accounting bias in post-merger profitability, since the difference between $V.2$ and $V.3$ is the distorting element in the profitability calculation, goodwill. A procedure has therefore been developed for estimating the goodwill arising on consolidation in order that allowance can be made for its effect on post-merger profitability.

This component of goodwill (G) is estimated as:

$$G = T15_{ay} - T15_{ay-1} - T38_{ay} - T80_{ay} \qquad \text{(A.i)}$$

Where:

a: acquirer.

y: year of acquisition.

$T15$: goodwill per balance sheet.

$T38$: increase in intangible assets per uses of funds statement (i.e. purchases of intangible assets other than goodwill on acquisition).

$T80$: goodwill in the accounts of the victim company at the time of takeover.

Lest this estimation procedure might produce extreme and inappropriate results because of odd treatments of goodwill by individual companies or D.I. analysts, the absolute value of G was constrained to be no greater than the absolute value of $(V.1 - V.3)$. It is possible that $V.2$ sometimes actually exceeded $V.1$, with the result that this estimate of G would be biased downwards; but given the accounting profession's predisposition to conservative valuation, it did not seem likely that the acquirer's book valuation of a subsidiary would exceed the market value too frequently, or by too much. Given the possibility of unforeseen and unwarranted extreme results if the constraint were not applied, the expedient seemed justifiable.

Profitability adjusted for the accounting bias on acquisition (F in chapter 3) was then defined as:

$$F_y = \frac{2.U_y}{D_y + D_{y-1} - G} \qquad \text{(A.ii)}$$

$$F_{y+1} = \frac{2.U_{y+1}}{D_{y+1} + D_y - 2G} \qquad \text{(A.iii)}$$

$$F_{y+2} = \frac{2.U_{y+2}}{D_{y+2} + D_{y+1} - 2G} \qquad \text{(A.iv)}$$

...etc.

Where U = profit ($T66 - T32 - T33 - T34 + T59$)

D = net assets ($T22$).

(See appendix B for definitions of variables in the 'T' sequence.)

5 This information on valuations has been obtained from the D.I.'s duplicated instructions prepared for the Department's staff responsible for the analysis and standardisation of the accounts in our Data Bank; and from discussions with the Department's staff, Mrs W.R. Borland and Mr P.G. Reeve.

Table A.A   Profitability according to the standard measure and profitability adjusted for the accounting bias: G.E.C. in 1968

Principally as a result of the takeover of A.E.I., goodwill on consolidation of some £170 million was added to the net assets of G.E.C. in 1968, apart from the addition of the net assets of the new subsidiaries at historic cost.

According to the estimation procedure detailed above,

$G = £170.6m^a$

This figure was used to obtain an adjusted profitability figure for 1968 and subsequent years using (A.ii, A.iii, etc.).

	R	F
1968	12.9%	15.6%
1969	10.2	13.7
1970	10.5	13.9
1971	12.2	16.0

[a] The goodwill figure given by Lee (1974) for the takeover of A.E.I. alone which was obtained from a detailed examination of the company's accounts was £167.1m. The small difference is probably due to goodwill arising on the other two minor acquisitions by G.E.C. in the same year.

Except that, if a company wrote off goodwill in a year succeeding the acquisition, and the total which was written off exceeded G, then it was assumed that it was the goodwill arising on consolidation which had been written off; and G rather than $2G$ was deducted from the denominator for the year of write-off with no goodwill deduction in subsequent years.

Comparison of adjusted with unadjusted profitability: an example

Table A.A. illustrates the potential scale of the accounting bias by comparing profitability according to the usual definition $(2U_y/(D_y + D_{y-1}))$ with F for the acquirer in a famous takeover of the late sixties, G.E.C.'s purchase of A.E.I. Profitability after allowance for the accounting bias is around a sixth higher than the conventional measure in the year of acquisition, and about a third higher in subsequent years. Consequently, if adjusted profitability (F) after the takeover were as high or even marginally higher than that achieved on average by the two companies prior to the takeover, tests based on the conventional measure of profitability alone (R) would reveal a marked decline in this performance indicator for G.E.C.

The typical extent of the accounting bias

To see whether G.E.C.'s experience was typical, or whether the accounting bias was by and large slight, the premia over book value and their effect on the conventional profitability measure were estimated for all acquisitions of quoted companies analysed by the D.I. between 1964 and 1971.[6]

Table A.B illustrates the relationship between the three valuation methods outlined above (V.1, the D.I. valuation (market in this period); V.2, the valuation in the acquirer's books; and V.3, the valuation in the victim's books). Goodwill arising on consolidation (V.2 − V.3) and the excess of market over victim's book value (V.1 − V.3) are expressed as percentages of the victim's book value. Though they are provided for reference, the relationships between the aggregate (all acquisitions) values

6   See the D.I.'s criteria for analysing takeovers, discussed above.

Table A.B Alternative valuations of new subsidiaries

	Book value of victims in their own books, prior to acquisition B^a £ million	Goodwill arising on consolidation G^b £ million	Excess of D.I.'s valuation over book value P^c £ million	$G \div B$ %	$P \div B$ %	Average of individual values of (G/B) for each acquirer g %	Average of individual values of (P/B) for each acquirer p %
1964 (60)	387.1	87.8^d	60.9	22.7	15.7	36.4	46.6
1965 (70)	362.0	16.5	35.6	4.6	9.8	31.7	58.3
1966 (55)	315.0	44.6	46.5	14.2	14.8	31.8	37.9
1967 (68)	729.5	38.2^d	31.5	5.2	4.3	21.4	30.6
1968 (120)	1055.2	205.8	584.4	19.5	55.4	34.0	68.4
1969 (91)	612.2	125.8	204.9	20.6	33.5	30.8	67.3
1970 (86)	553.3	52.5	77.1	9.5	13.9	31.4	45.7
1971 (46)	526.2	113.0	249.0	21.5	47.3	34.9	73.6

Notes:
a. Equal to V.3 (see above).
b. Equal to V.2 − V.3.
c. Equal to V.1 − V.3
d. G exceeds P in aggregate in two years even though it is constrained not to exceed the absolute value of P, because P takes on negative values more frequently.

The number of acquirers contributing to the total is given in brackets under the year.

The sum of B and P falls short of the aggregate expenditure by quoted companies on acquisitions detailed in Department of Industry (1975). This is because acquirers which bought small subsidiaries whose accounts were not analysed by the D.I. have not been included in the estimates provided in this table. These exclusions are of minor significance, however: the aggregate of $(P + B)$ is very close to the published totals in all years.

of these variables are not the most relevant in assessing the likely impact of the valuation bias on profitability: they depend to a great extent on the accounting treatment of a small number of takeovers which dominate the aggregates (the size distribution of companies, and hence of takeover victims exhibiting high positive skewness). The studies of takeover's influence on profitability, reported above, give each company equal weight: so it is appropriate here to calculate the ratio of good-will and market premium to book value for each individual acquiring firm, and then take simple averages of these values across companies. The resulting statistics are provided in the final columns of Table A.B.

The premium of market over book value is considerable, of the order of one to two-thirds of book value. Moreover, being very sensitive to the general level of stock market prices, it fluctuates considerably between years. This illustrates the shortcomings of this measure as a guide to year to year changes in the volume of takeover activity.

The goodwill recorded in the acquirer's books, the key variable in estimating the bias in profitability, is appreciably lower than the market premium (it is of course constrained to be no greater — see above); but it is still around a third of book value. It also fluctuates much less violently than the market premium, so that any bias which it produces in profitability measures is unlikely to vary a great deal between mergers undertaken in different years.

Table A.C. reports the effect on profitability of this goodwill increment to the assets of an amalgamation. In the year of acquisition, adjusted profitability (with G deducted from the denominator) was typically between about 1% and $3\frac{1}{2}$% higher than unadjusted profitability. In the subsequent year (when $2G$ is deducted from the denominator), the difference ranged between 1.3% and 5.5%. Of course, for a persistent acquirer the difference would be cumulative and could far exceed these averages: these estimates include the effects of only a single year's acquisition activity.

Revaluation of tangible fixed assets

Companies may sometimes choose to revalue the fixed assets of the new subsidiary rather than create goodwill in the parent's balance sheet. However, Lee's (1974) study of company accounting practices upon merger suggests that this procedure is unusual. Moreover, the revaluation of fixed assets is not restricted to acquiring companies and may be undertaken by firms relying entirely on internal growth, thus also affecting chapter 3's yardstick measure, the industry profit rate. To bias the results, in the way that goodwill arising on consolidation certainly does, revaluation would have to be more important for the set of acquiring companies than for the rest with whom they were being compared. But a limited test does not confirm this possibility. For those among the acquirers studied in chapter 3 which made their takeover within the same 2 digit industry between 1964 and 1969, revaluations totalled 2% of 1969 net assets, whereas revaluations for all the companies which continued from 1964–9 amounted during this period to 3.5% of their 1969 net assets. It must be admitted that, especially prior to the 1967 Companies Act, information on revaluations was not perfect and universally available, and that this test is less than comprehensive; but it certainly does not suggest that the results of chapter 3 would be challenged were the effect of revaluations to be successfully eliminated from the profitability measures for both acquiring companies and the rest of the population.

Table A.C   The effect on profitability of goodwill arising on consolidation

Year of acquisition	Adjusted profitability ÷ Raw profitability (%) Year of takeover[a]	Subsequent year[b]	Number of acquirers	Number of acquirers surviving to subsequent year
1964	102.32 (0.50)	103.34 (1.00)	60	58
1965	102.23 (0.45)	103.52 (1.02)	70	69
1966	100.80 (0.05)	101.35 (0.11)	55	52
1967	101.27 (0.15)	102.31 (0.41)	68	63
1968	103.38 (1.07)	105.55 (2.65)	120	117
1969	102.90 (0.68)	103.82 (1.27)	91	76
1970	101.71 (0.22)	102.67 (0.56)	86	85
1971	103.68 (1.11)	103.83 (0.54)	46	15

Notes:
[a] Adjusted profitability for the year of acquisition as defined above (A.ii).
[b] Adjusted profitability for the year after acquisition as defined above (A.iii).

Raw profitability in year j is always defined as $2U_j/(D_j + D_{j-1})$ (U being profit, and D net assets).

The standard deviation of each ratio is given in brackets beneath the mean of the ratio.

Appendix B. The population, the data and detailed definitions of variables used in the study

Introduction
This appendix provides some description of the data bank on which most of the study is based. It reports the data bank's coverage and its limitations (and refers to other sources of such information). In addition it provides a full listing of the quantitative variables included, grouped within their balancing accounts. Then detailed definitions of variables drawn from the data bank and used in the study are provided.

Scope of the data bank
The population incorporated in the data bank was defined at the beginning of the period to include all companies engaged primarily in manufacturing, distributive trades and some other services, and having stocks and shares quoted on United Kingdom stock exchanges. From 1948 to 1960 about 2500 companies typically qualified for inclusion on this criterion (the number varying from year to year as a result of births and deaths). From 1960, however, the population was truncated. Those with net assets of less than £0.5 million and gross income of less than £50,000 in 1960 or 1964 were excluded in subsequent years. The total number of companies covered by the data fell from 2618 to 2241 as a result of the exclusions in 1960. From 1969, companies with net assets of less than £2 million or gross income of less than £200,000 were excluded: a loss of some 350 companies. Though these excluded companies numbered many, however, their aggregate size was very small in relation to the total for quoted companies. Data were incorporated in the data bank for all eligible companies for every year from 1948 to 1971; and are included for some for 1972 as well.

Each 'company-year' of data contains the company's financial accounts, supplemented by various biographical details. These biographical details are recorded in 25 'indicative' variables. The financial accounts comprise a balance sheet, income appropriation account and sources and uses of funds statement (totalling 67 'quantitative' variables). For years from 1964, up to a further 83 quantitative variables are available to augment the basic accounting information.

In all then the data bank contains some 6 million items of information. As for the economic significance of this population, in 1970 it accounted for around 75% of the gross trading profits of all companies in the United Kingdom; and its operations generated around 25% of G.N.P.[1]

1 Sources: Department of Industry (1973) and Central Statistical Office (1972).

Sources of the data

The published accounts of eligible companies were collected and arranged in a standard format first by the National Institute of Economic and Social Research and then by the Board of Trade (now Department of Industry (D.I.)). Up to 1963 these bodies transferred the data to punched card; the Department of Applied Economics at Cambridge subsequently transferred much of the data from punched cards to magnetic tape, a job completed by the Department of Accounting and Business Method at Edinburgh University. This department also obtained data from the D.I. for years after 1964, developed a single format for the diversely arranged sets of data for different periods, extracted further information from the D.I.'s non-computerised records to augment the data bank,[2] and investigated and corrected inaccuracies or omissions revealed by a programme of tests of the completed data bank.[3]

Remaining shortcomings of the data

These may be summarised:

(i)   *Non-comparable data for different years*

Firstly, the legal disclosure requirements for companies were changed in the 1967 Companies Act.[4] This caused one or two detailed account headings to be non-comparable; but generally produced welcome additional information to supplement that already required. Secondly, the D.I. has made major changes to the scope of the information which they included in their standardised accounts — especially in 1964 and 1969 — which means that some information in the data bank is available only for later years of the period. Some of these changes were a response to the changes in company disclosure requirements (see above); while others (e.g. the additional information provided on takeovers from 1964: see appendix A) were entirely on the initiative of the D.I. Thirdly, the D.I. made a major change in valuation methods in 1964 affecting external finance raised in the course of takeover (see appendix A). Finally, changes in the definitions of variables were prompted by developments in the institutional setting — for instance the introduction or abandonment of differential rates of taxation for dividends and retentions (see Meeks and Whittington (1976), appendix B), and the introduction of the investment grant system (see Department of Accounting and Business Method (1974)).

(ii)   *Deficiencies of historic cost accounting*

The drawbacks of conventional historic cost accounts have been much publicised and debated in recent years. New proposals have been produced for alternative accounting methods, first by the accounting profession (Accounting Standards Steering Committee (1973) and (1974)) and then by a committee

2 These included data on taxation and dividends under the arrangements for transition to the Corporation Tax System; on investment grants; on the causes of death of companies with incomplete records; on the identity of the acquirer (for the merger study in chapter 3); and company names, as well as the repair of detailed omissions in the existing computer file (see Department of Accounting and Business Method (1974) for more detail).

3 This work was carried out by the author and G. Whittington, with Mrs A.G. Harris programming the computer. Details of tests carried out, etc. are provided in Department of Accounting and Business Method (1974).

4 For the disclosure requirements of the Companies Acts, see Chartered Accountants' Trust for Education and Research (1967).

76

established by the government (Sandilands Committee (1975)); and reform is imminent. The main impetus to reform is that under inflation some form of current cost valuation of assets is deemed preferable for certain purposes to historic cost valuation. In particular, vigorous debate has developed over whether it is appropriate to count as income stock appreciation and the shortfall of historic below current cost depreciation.

These issues are not trivial in recent years (see the estimates in Meeks (1974)), but they were certainly less acute in the period covered by this study (ending around 1971) than in the subsequent period of very rapid inflation. Moreover, for the main section of this study (chapter 3), some of the problems are minimised, if not avoided: the chief comparison is between the pre- and post-merger experience of the same (amalgamated) company. And while an income or asset measure might differ from a preferred measure throughout the study period for this company, there is generally no presumption that the extent of the difference will change upon merger, to vitiate the comparison. Where there is such a presumption, of course, as in the case of goodwill created upon merger, explicit adjustment is made to allow for its effect (see appendix A).

(iii)   *Inadequate disclosure by companies*
The 1967 Companies Act remedied some of the glaring omissions of data which are crucial in much economic analysis of company accounts – for instance of sales data. But, for instance, the sources and uses of funds statement is not yet a compulsory component of companies' published accounts; and those in the data bank are estimates derived from the other financial statements and other sources apart from companies' accounts (see appendix A). Again, the disclosure of the valuation and accounting treatment of takeovers leaves something to be desired (see appendix A).

(iv)   *Differences between companies in accounting practice*
Some such differences defy the D.I. analysts' attempts to standardise companies' accounts. For instance, the interpretation of historic cost may vary between companies – especially in the valuation of stocks; companies variously capitalise or treat as current costs such items as research and development expenditure; and the lease or rent of fixed assets sometimes takes the place of outright purchase of such assets.

Many of these shortcomings are dealt with to some extent (and the data adjusted) where they impinge on the analysis (this is especially true of items (i) and (ii)). Where they are expected to produce a bias in the results but no allowance is made explicitly for the bias, the result is qualified in the text. But the continuing debate over which measures of income and assets are appropriate, and the disturbances in values for the measures actually used do warn against too precise interpretation of many of the results.[5]

---

5   More detailed discussion of the problems associated with these accounting data are provided in Singh and Whittington (1968), appendix A, and Meeks and Whittington (1976), appendix B. Discussion of particular problems in standardising these data is developed in Department of Accounting and Business Method (1974) and of general issues in standardising accounts in Weaver (1971). At a more general level still are the discussions of interpreting company accounts in Bird (1971) and Parker (1972).

Detailed definitions of variables used in the study
Notation

m = last year of period
p = first year of period
o = p minus 1
n = number of years in the period
j = year indicator

A number prefixed with 'T' represents an accounting variable from Table B.A.

Table 2.A
Expenditure on new subsidiaries = $T39_j$
Expenditure on gross new investment = $T37_j$
Expenditure on net new investment = $(T37 - T32 - T33)_j$
Each variable is aggregated across all companies

Table 2.B
The general definition is:

$$\sum_{j=p}^{m} Q_j \div n$$

Where: $Q_j = (T37 - T32 - T33)_j \div T22_{j-1}$
(Net new investment in fixed assets)

$$Q_j = (T38 + T40 + T41 + T42 + T43 + T44 + T45 + T46 + T47$$
$$+ T48 + T49 - T27 - T28 - T29 - T30)_j \div T22_{j-1}$$

(Acquisition of net current assets, etc.)

$$Q_j = T39_j \div T22_{j-1}$$

(Acquisition of subsidiaries: for cash and by share for share exchange; this is the definition normally used in the book for growth by acquisition.)

$$Q_j = [(T7 + T8)_j - (T7 + T8)_{j-1} - T26_j] \div T22_{j-1}$$

(Acquisition of subsidiaries: by taking on minority interests and long-term liabilities of subsidiaries.)

$$Q_j = (T32 + 33)_j \div T22_{j-1}$$

(Depreciation and 'replacement investment'.)

Table 2.C
As for Table 2.B

Equation (3.i), Table 3.A, etc.

$$N = T66 - T32 - T33 - T34 + T59$$

(Pre-tax profit)

$$D = T60 + T7 + T8 - T4 = T22$$

(Net assets: the usual size measure used in the study.)

Table 4.B
The general definition is:

$$\sum_{j=p}^{m} Q_j \div n$$

Where: $Q_j = (T31 + T35 + T36 - T43)_j \div T22_{j-1}$

(Growth by retentions)

$Q_j = [(T23 + T24 + T7 + T8)_j - (T7 + T8)_{j-1}] \div T22_{j-1}$

(Growth by external finance)

$Q_j = (T68 + T69 + T70)_j \div T22_{j-1}$

(Issues of shares and loans in exchange)

Minority interests, etc. assumed on acquiring subsidiaries are defined above for Table 2.B; so too is total expenditure on subsidiaries: retentions used to buy subsidiaries are then obtained by deducting from total expenditure on subsidiaries these two components of external finance raised in the course of acquisition. Net investment in fixed and working capital is defined for Table 2.B. Retentions expended on this item are obtained by deducting from this total the external finance raised for cash, for which:

$$Q_j = (T23 + T24 + T26 - T68 - T69 - T70)_j \div T22_{j-1}$$

Net and replacement investment (depreciation) are defined for Table 2.B.

Tables 4.C and 4.D
The variables are defined just as for Tables 2.B and 4.B; instead of averages across all companies in the population, averages for the sub-groups of the population are computed.

Table 5.A
Size (net assets) is defined as for equation (3.i) above.

Table 5.B
Net new investment is as defined for Table 2.B. Gross new investment is similarly defined, except that:

$$Q_j = T37_j \div T22_{j-1}$$

Table 5.C
The variables are as defined for Tables 2.B and 5.B.

Tables C.C and D.A
The variables are as defined for Tables 2.B and 4.C.

Tables D.B and D.G

The variables for these tables are mostly as defined for Tables 2.B, 4.B, etc. In addition the following variables are used:

$$\sum_{j=p}^{m} Q_j \div n$$

Where:

$$Q_j = (T39 - T88 - T89 - T92 - T93)_j \div T22_{j-1}$$

(Rate of growth by takeover at book value.)

$$Q_j = (T68 + T69 + T70)_j \div T22_{j-1}$$

(Rate of growth by external finance: in exchange for subsidiaries.)

$$Q_j = (T23 + T24 + T26 - T68 - T69 - T70)_j \div T22_{j-1}$$

(Rate of growth by external finance: for cash.)

Tables D.C and D.H

The general definition is:

$$\sum_{j=p}^{m} H_j \div \sum_{j=p}^{m} Y_j$$

Where $Y_j = (T23 + T24 + T26 + T32 + T33 + T35)_j$

and $H_j = (T23 - T68)_j$	Issues of ordinary shares: for cash*
$T68_j$	Issues of ordinary shares: in exchange*
$T23_j$	Issues of ordinary shares: total
$(T24 - T69)_j$	Issues of preference shares: for cash*
$T69_j$	Issues of preference shares: in exchange*
$T24_j$	Issues of preference shares: total
$(T26 - T70)_j$	Issues of long-term loans: for cash*
$T70_j$	Issues of long-term loans: in exchange*
$T26_j$	Issues of long-term loans: total
$T35_j$	Retentions
$(T32 + T33)_j$	Depreciation $\equiv$ Replacement investment
$(T37 - T32 - T33)_j$	Net fixed investment, tangible
$T38_j$	Intangible fixed investment
$T39_j$	Investment in subsidiaries, etc.
$T40_j$	Increase in stocks
$(T47 + T48 + T49 - T27)_j$	Increase in bank balances, etc.
$(T41 - T28)_j$	Increase in trade credit
$(T42 + T43 + T44 + T45 + T46 - T25 - T29 - T30 - T31 - T34 - T36)_j$	Other current and sundry

*Not available before 1964.

Tables D.D and D.I

The general definition is:

$$\sum_{j=p}^{m} N_j \div \sum_{j=p}^{m} Z_j$$

Where $Z_j = (T50 + T51 + T52)_j$

and $N_j = (T32 + T33 + T34)_j$	Depreciation, etc.
$(T50 - T32 - T33 - T34)_j$	Operating profit
$T51_j$	Dividends and interest received
$T52_j$	Other income
$T53_j$	Interest paid
$(T57 - T59)_j$	Minority interests and prior-year adjustment
$T35_j$	Retentions

The definitions of taxation and of dividend payments were subject to special procedures to achieve consistency between tax systems. These lengthy procedures are detailed in Meeks and Whittington (1976); they are not repeated here since these particular variables are not specially emphasised in the analysis.

Tables D.E., D.F., D.J., and D.K
The general definition is:
$G_o \div T22_o$ (opening balance sheet) $G_m \div T22_m$ (closing balance sheet)

Where G —

$T1$	Ordinary shares
$T3$	Reserves
$T2$	Preference shares
$T8$	Long-term loans
$T5$	Future tax
$T7$	Minority interests
$T14$	Fixed assets: tangible
$T15$	Fixed assets: intangible
$T16$	Fixed assets: trade investments
$T17$	Stocks
$(T19 + T20 + T21 - T9)$	Net liquidity
$(T18 - T10 - T11 - T12 - T4)$	Other current and sundry

Extreme values
The procedure adopted for dealing with extreme values in the single merger study is discussed in chapter 3. A comparable problem also arises in the exercises using all continuing companies. And so that group averages would not be very seriously distorted by outliers, individual annual growth or profit rates were constrained to be no greater than 100% or less than -100%. In addition, companies which otherwise qualified for inclusion in the continuing populations were excluded when an individual item in the accounts reported in appendix D exceeded 200% of the sum of the account. 2.4% of continuing companies were excluded on this score for the first period (31 companies, leaving 1250) and 5.3% for the second period (54 companies leaving 966).

Table B.A   The quantitative data

Reference number 'T'	Name	Years available
	Capital and reserves	
1	Issued capital: ordinary	48–
2	Issued capital: preference	48–
3	Capital and revenue reserves	48–
4	Provisions	48–63
5	Future tax reserves	48–
	Memorandum	
6	Contracts for capital expenditure outstanding	48–
	Liabilities	
7	Interest of minority shareholders in subsidiaries	48–63
8	Long-term liabilities	48–
9	Bank overdrafts and loans	48–
10	Trade and other creditors	48–
11	Dividends and interest liabilities	48–
12	Current taxation liabilities	48–
	Memorandum	
13	Total depreciation	48–
	Assets	
14	Fixed assets: tangible, net of depreciation	48–
15	Fixed assets: intangible	48–
16	Fixed assets: trade investments	48–
17	Stocks and work in progress	48–
18	Trade and other debtors	48–
19	Marketable securities	48–
20	Tax reserve certificates	48–
21	Cash	48–
	Summary	
22	Total net assets	48–
	Sources of funds	
23	Issue of shares: ordinary	49–
24	Issue of shares: preference	49–
25	Increase in liability to minority interests	49–63 69–
26	Issue of long-term loans	49–
27	Bank credit received	49–
28	Trade and other credit received	49–
29	Increase in dividend and interest liabilities	49–
30	Increase in current tax liabilities	49–
31	Increase in future tax reserves	49–
32	Balance of profit: depreciation provision	49–
33	Balance of profit: provision for amortisation	49–63
34	Balance of profit: other provisions	49–63
35	Balance of profit: retained in reserves	49–
36	Other receipts	49–

Table B.A   The quantitative data

Reference number 'T'	Name	Years available
	Uses of funds	
37	Expenditure, less receipts, on fixed assets – tangible	49–
38	Expenditure, less receipts, on fixed assets – intangible	49–
39	Expenditure, less receipts, on fixed assets – trade investments and subsidiaries	49–
40	Increase in value of stocks and work in progress	49–
41	Increase in credit given – trade and other debtors	49–
42	Expenditure ex provisions	49–63 69–
43	Sundry expenditure	49–
	Adjustments	
44	Consolidation adjustment	49–
45	Conversion adjustment	49–63
46	Residual adjustment	49–63
	Balance	
47	Change in securities	49–
48	Change in tax reserve certificates	49–
49	Change in cash	49–
	Appropriation of income	
50	Operating profit (before depreciation)	49–
51	Dividends and interest received (gross of income tax)	49–
52	Other income	49–
53	Interest paid on long-term liabilities gross	49–
54	Tax on current profit	49–
55	Dividend, ordinary	49–
56	Dividend, other	49–
57	To minority interests in subsidiaries, net of taxation	49–63
58	Prior year adjustments – tax	49–
59	Prior year adjustments – general	49–
	Summary	
60	Total capital and reserves	48–
61	Total liabilities	48–
62	Total fixed assets, net of depreciation	48–
63	Total current assets	48–
64	Total sources	49–
65	Total uses	49–
66	Total profit	49–
67	Total balance of profit	49–

Table B.A   The quantitative data

Reference number 'T'	Name	Years available
	Expenditure on acquiring subsidiaries: consideration for subsidiaries acquired	
68	Ordinary shares	64–
69	Preference, etc. shares	64–
70	Long-term loans	64–
71	Cash	64–
72	Previous holding added back	64–
73	Total consideration	64–
	Excess payment	
74	Number of companies: accounts analysed	64–
75	Number of companies: accounts not analysed	64–
	Excess book value	
76	Number of companies: accounts analysed	64–
77	Number of companies: accounts not analysed	64–
	Companies acquired (accounts analysed)	
78	Number of companies	64–
79	Net tangible fixed assets	64–
80	Goodwill, etc.	64–
81	Investments	64–
82	Current assets (excluding investments)	64–
83	Unidentified assets	64–
84	Less: minority interests	64–
85	deferred tax reserves	64–
86	long-term loans	64–
87	current liabilities	64–
	Payment less book value	
88	Excess payment	64–
89	Excess book value	64–
	Companies acquired (accounts not analysed)	
90	Book value	64–
91	Number of companies	64–
	Payment less book value	
92	Excess payment	64–
93	Excess book value	64–
	Unconsolidated companies acquired	
94	Assumed book value	64–
95	Number of companies	64–
96	Proceeds from sales of subsidiaries	64–
97	Amount written off subsidiaries	64–
98	Further investment in subsidiaries	64–
99	Upward revaluation of subsidiaries	64–

Table B.A   The quantitative data

Reference number 'T'	Name	Years available
	Investment grants	
100	Increase in investment grant reserve	
101	Transfer to profit and loss account	
102	Transfer to tax equalisation account	
103	Direct credit to profit and loss	
104	Amount deducted from fixed assets	
105	Other treatments	
106	Increase in investment grants due but unpaid	
107	Investment grants received	
	Miscellaneous extra information	
108	Investment grant reserve	69–
109	Asset replacement reserve	69–
110	Pension fund	69–
111	Tax equalisation reserve	69–
112	Debentures and mortgages	69–
113	Provisions	69–
114	Land and buildings gross of depreciation	64–
115	Plant, etc. gross of depreciation	64–
116	Total gross tangible assets	64–
117	Depreciation: land and buildings	64–
118	Depreciation: plant, etc.	64–
119	Cash paid for subsidiaries	64–
120	Quoted investments	69–
121	Market value of quoted investments	69–
122	Income from quoted investments	69–
123	Expenditure on hire of plant	68–
124	Overseas tax on profits of year	69–
125	Transfer to tax equalisation reserve and other deferred tax	69–
126	Transfer to asset replacement reserve	69–
127	Sales	68–
128	Exports	68–
129	Intangible assets: development and other deferred revenue expenditure	68–
130	Change in accumulated depreciation	68–
131	Change in deferred tax reserve	68–
132	Change in fixed assets due to revaluation	68–
133	Change in fixed assets due to currency devaluation	68–
134	Average number of employees	68–
135	Employees remuneration	68–
136	Total directors' pay	68–
137	Chairman's pay	69–
138	Highest paid director's pay	69–
	Directors' in the following income bands	
139	0 – 2500	
140	2501 – 5000	
141	5001 – 7500	
142	7501 – 10000	

Table B.A   The quantitative data

Reference number 'T'	Name	Years available
143	10001 − 20000	
144	20001 − 30000	
145	30001 − 40000	
146	40001 − 50000	
147	Over 50,000	
148	Schedule F payable	1965
149	Transitional tax relief: ordinary dividends	1966
150	Transitional tax relief: preference dividends	1966

Appendix C. Further evidence in support of chapter 3

Survey of earlier work on the impact of merger on company performance[1]
Of the three earlier studies which incorporate profitability as a success criterion, Singh's (1971) is closest in method to that reported here (the method used was in part modelled on his). He asks what proportion of his sample of 77 acquiring companies performed less well after the merger than did the two participants prior to the merger. In fact a majority showed a decline in profitability. True, it considers records for only 2 years after merger, and the results are now becoming rather old (they relate to the nineteen-fifties: see Table C.A. for a summary of the coverage and results of earlier studies). Nevertheless, its results do closely resemble those produced in chapter 3 for more recent years; moreover, the pattern he reported for the immediate post-merger years is found to persist over longer periods.

A study for the United States (Lev and Mandelker, 1972) and one for Britain (Utton, 1974) both match acquisitive (active in takeover) with non-acquisitive companies of similar size and (in the former case only) from the same industry. The former study finds little difference in the profitability records of the two groups; while Utton reports that the merging companies were markedly inferior on this criterion. That neither study made allowance for the accounting bias discussed in appendix A prompts some reservations about these conclusions, and Utton shows some concern that he made no allowance for the influence of industry on his samples of acquiring and non-acquiring firms. However, there is no presumption that the latter influence would weaken the conclusions; and the disparity in performance between merging and non-merging companies is so big that the accounting bias would have to be very considerable to alter the results qualitatively (see chapter 3).[2]

Lev and Mandelker also compared the two groups' performance in terms of dividends plus the appreciation in their share price. By contrast with the results for profitability the acquirers achieved superiority according to this criterion. A second study which revealed divergent movements in earnings and in the share price was that of Kelly (1967): he compared the records of 22 merging companies with those of 22 non-merging companies which had been matched with the acquirers on the

---

1 This survey owes a good deal to Utton's (1974) work. This account is included because it gives much more emphasis than Utton's to the choice of performance measure and the distribution of gains and losses upon merger, factors which could seriously affect the efficiency conclusions which may be drawn from some of the studies.
2 As background information on the influence of industry, simple averages of rates of profit and of growth by acquisition for the companies within each of 23 2 digit industries are given in Table C.C.

Table C.A Summary of earlier work on the relationship between merger and performance

The performance variable relates to the acquiring company except where stated. The study is for the United States except where stated.

Author	Period	Sample Size	Yardstick	Performance measure	Verdict
Singh	1954–60 (U.K.)	77	Participants' earlier profitability, in relation to industry.	Rate of return on net assets.	Unfavourable
Utton	1961–70 (U.K.)	39	Matched sample (with respect to size).	Rate of return on net assets.	Unfavourable
Lev and Mandelker	1947–68	69	Matched sample (with respect to size and industry).	Rates of return on total and on equity assets.	Indecisive
				Dividends plus share price appreciation.	Favourable
Kelly	1946–60	22	Matched sample (with respect to size and industry).	Change in share price.	Indecisive
				Change in price-earnings ratio.	Favourable
				Change in earnings per share.	Unfavourable
Hogarty	1953–64	43	Industry average.	Dividends plus share price increase.	Unfavourable
				Change in earnings per share.	Indecisive
Lorie and Halpern	1955–67	115	Market index.	Victim shareholders' capital appreciation.	Favourable
Ryden	1955–68 (Sweden)	54	Tested for individual industries.	Relation of share price increase to: one acquisition rate;	Positive
				alternative acquisition rate.	Indecisive
Reid	1951–61	478	Tested for individual industries.	Relation to acquisition rate of: change in share price.	Negative
				change in earnings per unit of opening assets;	Negative
				change in earnings per unit of opening sales.	Negative

basis of industry and size. The two groups' share price performed equally well, though the merging companies enjoyed a greater improvement in their price-earnings ratio; necessarily, therefore, the merging companies performed less well in terms of the change in earnings per share. Thus in both these studies it appears that the advantage displayed by the acquirers stemmed from shareholders' bidding up their share price to an extent that was not obviously justified by their current performance.

Three other studies concentrate on a stock market indicator of merging companies' performance. Hogarty (1970) used a common measure of shareholder gains to assess the success of merger, comparing the dividends plus share price appreciation of 43 merging companies with the industry average of the same measure. Only 3 merging companies achieved clear success on this criterion, whilst 21 failed (the rest falling in the twilight). A second comparison, using the improvement in earnings per share as the success measure, was quite inconclusive. Lorie and Halpern (1970) examined the capital record of shareholders in a specific set of victim companies: those where the shareholders were paid in 'funny money' — convertible preferred stock, etc. (not cash, common stock and ordinary bonds). They found that capital appreciation for those holders typically outpaced the market index.[3] Finally, Ryden (1972) related the improvement in share price to the acquisition rate for 54 Swedish companies. On one measure of the acquisition rate, he found a positive association, whilst, on another, the association disappeared.

Two difficulties hinder the use of studies which measure success in terms of share price movements in a discussion of the efficiency consequences of merger. Firstly, there is the possibility suggested by the work of Lev and Mandelker and of Kelly that acquiring companies could be valued more highly than their performance would seem to justify — perhaps as the result of some irrational stock market fashion. Secondly, all the studies of this type which are reviewed here focus on the experience of one partner in the takeover bargain, not distinguishing the general gains in profitability brought about by the merger from gains or losses associated with the exchange terms between the acquirer's and the victim's shares. In fact, in a particular merger, if the capital market is imperfect, the acquirer's shareholders might lose (as Reid (1968) found),[4] and the victim's gain (as Lorie and Halpern found), whilst the rate of profit on total capital employed was unchanged (as Lev and Mandelker found). It would be misleading, therefore, to lend equal weight to all the diverse results as if each measure were an equally valid, unambiguous proxy

3 Jones, Tweedie and Whittington (1976) also found that the shareholders of takeover victims enjoyed above average returns in terms of dividends plus capital appreciation.
4 Reid was concerned with the role of merger in the growth-profitability trade-off hypothesised by the managerial theorists of the firm (and discussed in chapter 3). He related various growth and earnings measures to the frequency of merger. On the earnings side he measured the proportionate increase in the share price and in profits that could be attributed to the original shareholders. Whether the observations were pooled or segregated by industry, he found a negative association between merger-intensity and these performance measures. At first sight these tests seem to resemble those in chapter 3, in relating the change in profit to the rate of growth by acquisition; but in fact they too suffer from the problems of those studies using share prices as indices of performance. For Reid's device for allocating the change in profit to the original shareholders means that an unfavourable change in profit on his measurement could be the result not of poor profitability performance but of unfavour-able share exchange terms for the acquirer's shareholders (a situation consistent with the evidence of Lorie and Halpern and of Jones, Tweedie and Whittington).

for the profitability, let alone the efficiency, consequences of merger. The three studies which select the rate of profit on total capital are the really useful ones for the issue raised in chapter 3;[5] and these all provide support for the finding of chapter 3 that merger did not typically result in improvements in profitability.

Three other studies of a different type have reached sceptical conclusions on the efficiency consequences of mergers. Two (Kitching (1967) and Newbould (1970)) are based on interviews with the managers of acquiring companies. Managers typically admitted that negligible gains or else actual losses in efficiency followed many mergers; and Newbould concluded that 'management appears to be the only consistent gainer from merger activity' (p. 192).[6] Finally, the case study treatment of mergers in particular markets by Hart, Utton and Walshe (1973) also revealed evidence of managerial diseconomies following merger (p. 101).

5   This is not to say that the others are not appropriate to other issues — such as the attitude
    of the stock market to mergers.
6   See chapter 3 on the gains to managers from merger.

Supplementary results on merger and performance

Table C.B.   The standardised profitability of amalgamations, before and after merger

| | All cases | | | Extremes removed | | | | |
| | Raw profitability | | | Raw profitability | | Adjusted profitability | | |
Year	R	S_r	n	R	S_r	F	S_f	n
y^{-3}	1.208	3.198	233	1.057	0.263	1.057	0.263	213
y^{-2}	1.340	6.717	233	1.119	0.267	1.119	0.267	213
y^{-1}	1.165	0.542	233	1.138	0.219	1.138	0.219	213
y	1.276	1.143	233	1.218	0.296	1.252	0.322	213
y^{+1}	1.088	0.603	211	1.055	0.312	1.094	0.343	192
y^{+3}	0.738	10.422	191	1.064	0.268	1.088	0.287	174
y^{+3}	0.877	1.868	161	1.042	0.340	1.053	0.347	146
y^{+4}	1.095	3.854	113	0.994	0.327	0.995	0.323	103
y^{+5}	0.781	1.175	73	0.928	0.314	0.927	0.312	67
y^{+6}	0.823	0.551	50	0.959	0.313	0.961	0.315	44
y^{+7}	0.966	0.451	23	0.999	0.457	0.998	0.458	21

Notes:
See chapter 3 for full definitions.

R is unadjusted profitability as a proportion of profitability for the industry-year.

F is adjusted profitability as a proportion of profitability for the industry-year.

S is the standard deviation.

n is the number of cases surviving to that year, and incorporated in the averages.

Table C.C   The average rate of growth by acquisition of subsidiaries and the average rate of profit: by industry, 1964–71

| Industry | | Number of companies | % per annum | |
			Rate of growth by acquisition	Rate of profit
10	Mixed activities	1	6.6	10.3
21	Food	30	7.1	16.2
23	Drink	47	2.5	15.1
24	Tobacco	4	3.4	17.3
26	Chemicals	48	6.2	19.0
31	Metal manufacture	42	4.0	18.4
33	Non-electrical engineering	110	3.9	15.7
36	Electrical engineering	50	5.8	18.8
37	Shipbuilding	7	2.1	6.8
38	Vehicles	27	4.7	19.4
39	Metal goods, not elsewhere specified	68	4.1	19.1
41	Textiles	69	4.0	14.9
43	Leather, etc.	7	7.3	17.1
44	Clothing and footwear	31	5.8	18.2
46	Bricks, pottery, etc.	40	7.1	16.8
47	Timber, etc.	31	2.9	19.5
48	Paper, printing, etc.	55	4.4	15.1
49	Other manufacturing	38	4.4	19.3
50	Construction	49	7.7	20.1
70	Transport	16	3.7	16.0
81	Wholesale distribution	71	5.0	19.2
82	Retail distribution	79	3.1	19.6
88	Miscellaneous services	46	9.0	16.1
All companies		966	4.9	17.5

Notes:
For detailed definitions see appendix B.

Only companies which continued in independent existence within the population are included.

Table C.D   The standardised profitability of amalgamations, before and after merger: unadjusted profitability (diversification study)

Year	Same 3 digit			Other 3 digit			Other 2 digit		
	R	S_r	n	R	S_r	n	R	S_r	n
y^{-3}	0.982	0.300	102	1.119	0.244	30	1.128	0.241	81
y^{-2}	1.043	0.265	102	1.128	0.308	30	1.211	0.245	81
y^{-1}	1.062	0.203	102	1.172	0.185	30	1.220	0.242	81
y	1.190	0.295	102	1.153	0.367	30	1.279	0.274	81
y^{+1}	0.982	0.246	92	1.073	0.542	26	1.139	0.310	74
y^{+2}	1.002	0.235	82	0.984	0.309	25	1.169	0.283	67
y^{+3}	0.985	0.291	64	0.824	0.512	22	1.182	0.301	60
y^{+4}	1.004	0.276	48	0.707	0.288	13	1.071	0.380	42
y^{+5}	0.940	0.293	32	0.576	0.231	8	1.018	0.339	27
y^{+6}	0.855	0.302	22				1.036	0.314	21
y^{+7}	1.055	0.342	10				0.953	0.665	10

Notes:

See chapter 3 for full definitions.

R is raw profitability as a proportion of profitability for the industry-year.

S is the standard deviation.

n is the number of companies surviving to that year, and incorporated in the averages.

y is the year of merger.

Table C.E   The standardised profitability of amalgamations, before and after merger: adjusted profitability (diversification study)

Year	Same 3 digit			Other 3 digit			Other 2 digit		
	F	S_f	n	F	S_f	n	F	S_f	n
y^{-3}	0.982	0.300	102	1.119	0.244	30	1.128	0.241	81
y^{-2}	1.043	0.265	102	1.128	0.308	30	1.211	0.245	81
y^{-1}	1.062	0.203	102	1.172	0.185	30	1.220	0.242	81
y	1.229	0.330	102	1.207	0.407	30	1.298	0.284	81
y^{+1}	1.026	0.282	92	1.140	0.599	26	1.162	0.330	74
y^{+2}	1.024	0.258	82	1.032	0.329	25	1.187	0.300	67
y^{+3}	0.999	0.306	64	0.835	0.514	22	1.190	0.302	60
y^{+4}	0.997	0.265	48	0.715	0.292	13	1.078	0.382	42
y^{+5}	0.936	0.287	32	0.580	0.232	8	1.020	0.341	27
y^{+6}	0.855	0.303	22				1.039	0.316	21
y^{+7}	1.055	0.343	10				0.952	0.667	10

Notes:

See chapter 3 for full definitions.

F is adjusted profitability as a proportion of profitability for the industry-year.

S is the standard deviation.

n is the number of companies surviving to that year, and incorporated in the averages.

y is the year of merger.

Table C.F The standardised profitability of amalgamations, before and after merger: adjusted profitability (quartiles by X)

Year	Quartile A			Quartile B			Quartile C			Quartile D		
	R	S_r	n	R	S_r	n	R	S_r	n	R	S_r	n
y^{-3}	1.007	0.221	54	1.055	0.337	53	1.117	0.227	53	1.048	0.277	53
y^{-2}	1.087	0.196	54	1.106	0.356	53	1.204	0.295	53	1.081	0.226	53
y^{-1}	1.077	0.257	54	1.165	0.232	53	1.243	0.194	53	1.066	0.185	53
y	1.340	0.371	54	1.206	0.376	53	1.247	0.225	53	1.078	0.191	53
y^{+1}	0.994	0.252	47	1.056	0.432	48	1.147	0.317	50	1.017	0.250	47
y^{+2}	1.088	0.256	41	1.016	0.257	43	1.214	0.292	48	0.916	0.230	42
y^{+3}	1.014	0.384	34	0.964	0.442	32	1.182	0.334	44	0.966	0.208	36
y^{+4}	0.945	0.342	23	0.949	0.304	21	1.154	0.438	27	0.923	0.238	32
y^{+5}	0.856	0.338	13	0.913	0.306	13	1.061	0.348	17	0.880	0.306	24
y^{+6}	0.746	0.288	8	0.822	0.050	7	1.286	0.291	11	0.908	0.384	18
y^{+7}	0.443	0.335	5	0.820	0.121	3	1.290	0.374	6	1.222	0.530	7

Notes:
See chapter 3 for full definitions.

R is raw profitability as a proportion of profitability for the industry-year.

S is the standard deviation.

n is the number of companies surviving to that year, and incorporated in the averages.

y is the year of merger.

Table C.G The standardised profitability of amalgamations, before and after merger: adjusted profitability (quartiles by X)

Year	Quartile A			Quartile B			Quartile C			Quartile D		
	F	S_f	n	F	S_f	n	F	S_f	n	F	S_f	n
y^{-3}	1.007	0.221	54	1.055	0.337	53	1.117	0.227	53	1.048	0.277	53
y^{-2}	1.087	0.196	54	1.106	0.356	53	1.204	0.295	53	1.081	0.226	53
y^{-1}	1.077	0.257	54	1.165	0.232	53	1.243	0.194	53	1.066	0.185	53
y	1.396	0.398	54	1.248	0.427	53	1.270	0.232	53	1.092	0.199	53
y^{+1}	1.062	0.293	47	1.095	0.480	48	1.175	0.337	50	1.039	0.270	47
y^{+2}	1.132	0.299	41	1.035	0.263	43	1.232	0.301	48	0.935	0.252	42
y^{+3}	1.043	0.409	34	0.964	0.440	32	1.187	0.334	44	0.977	0.215	36
y^{+4}	0.944	0.342	23	0.949	0.293	21	1.148	0.428	27	0.932	0.243	32
y^{+5}	0.855	0.337	13	0.917	0.303	13	1.051	0.340	17	0.885	0.309	24
y^{+6}	0.744	0.288	8	0.827	0.051	7	1.284	0.294	11	0.912	0.387	18
y^{+7}	0.442	0.335	5	0.820	0.121	3	1.290	0.374	6	1.221	0.533	7

Notes:
See chapter 3 for full definitions.

F is adjusted profitability as a proportion of profitability for the industry-year.

S is the standard deviation.

n is the number of companies surviving to that year, and incorporated in the averages.

y is the year of merger.

Appendix D. Further evidence in support of chapters 4 and 5

Table D.A   Correlation coefficients: profitability with growth, 1964–71

Industry		Profitability with growth of net assets	Profitability with growth by net new investment	Profitability with growth by acqui-sition	Number of observations
21	Food	0.191	0.368	−0.146	30
23	Drink	0.412	0.412	0.117	49
26	Chemicals	0.531	0.453	0.222	49
31	Metal manufacture	0.525	0.509	0.096	43
33	Non-electrical engineering	0.513	0.364	0.003	117
36	Electrical engineering	0.220	0.205	−0.170	54
38	Vehicles	0.599	0.498	0.260	31
39	Metal goods, not else-where specified	0.268	0.240	0.008	70
41	Textiles	0.541	0.480	0.081	71
44	Clothing, footwear	0.812	0.726	0.569	33
46	Bricks, pottery, etc.	0.619	0.603	0.600	40
47	Timber, etc.	0.490	0.410	0.034	32
48	Paper, printing, etc.	0.614	0.547	−0.021	57
49	Other manufacturing	0.450	0.173	0.186	39
50	Construction	0.503	0.312	0.184	57
81	Wholesale distribution	0.608	0.560	0.226	78
82	Retail distribution	0.639	0.430	0.278	82
88	Miscellaneous services	0.364	0.169	0.183	49
All industries pooled:		0.488	0.368	0.156	1020

Notes:
Each of the variables is the arithmetic average of the corresponding ratio for each of the seven years, 1965–71 (1964 is the base year for the ratios).

See Appendix B for full definitions

The sum of observations for the individual industries falls short (by 39) of the total pooled observations: correlation coefficients were not estimated for industries with very few observations.

Table D.B Growth, financing ratios, etc.: analysis by expenditure on acquisitions.

	1948–64					1964–71				
Percentage per annum	Zero	Low	High	All companies	Top 100	Zero	Low	High	All companies	Top 100
Growth:										
of net assets[a]	6.4	6.9	12.0	9.0	21.0	6.3	7.5	18.9	11.8	37.2
by gross fixed investment[a]	6.3	6.9	8.6	7.5	11.8	7.9	9.2	11.6	8.9	14.6
by net fixed investment[a]	2.9	3.1	4.5	3.7	7.4	3.5	3.8	5.5	4.4	7.8
by takeover[a]: total	0	0.1	4.9	2.1	14.3	0	0.3	11.7	4.9	28.6
for cash	n.a.	n.a.	n.a.	n.a.	n.a.	0	0.1	4.2	1.7	7.9
by issue	n.a.	n.a.	n.a.	n.a.	n.a.	0	0.2	7.7	3.2	21.5
book value							0.1	8.4	3.4	19.6
by retention[a]	5.3	5.2	5.9	5.5	7.0	5.3	4.6	5.8	5.1	7.7
by external finance[a]: total	0.8	1.1	5.1	2.7	12.3	0.7	2.0	11.4	5.5	26.6
exchange	n.a.	n.a.	n.a.	n.a.	n.a.	0	0.2	7.7	3.2	21.6
Pre-tax rate of profit[b]	18.6	17.6	18.0	17.9	18.4	19.2	16.1	18.1	17.5	21.2
Opening size (£ million)	0.754	2.935	2.859	2.551	1.029	5.181	15.201	12.737	12.256	6.944
Number of companies	202	524	524	1250	100	188	388	390	966	100

Notes:
[a]Percentage of opening net assets.
[b]Percentage of average net assets.

See appendix B for fuller definitions.

Table D.C Sources and uses of funds: analysis by expenditure on acquisitions

	1948–64					1964–71				
	Zero	Low	High	All companies	Top 100	Zero	Low	High	All companies	Top 100
Sources of funds (%)										
Issues of ordinary shares:										
for cash						1.2	3.7	5.6	4.0	6.0
in exchange						0	1.5	18.4	8.0	35.6
total:	3.8	6.1	20.3	11.7	36.5	1.2	5.2	24.0	12.0	41.6
Issues of preference shares:										
for cash						−2.4	−0.5	−0.5	−0.9	0.4
in exchange						0	−0.1	0.5	0.2	1.1
total:	−0.4	0.2	1.5	0.7	3.0	−2.4	−0.4	0	−0.7	1.5
Issues of long-term loans:										
for cash						6.0	7.9	8.2	7.6	5.0
in exchange						0	0.4	6.4	2.7	12.0
total:	1.5	3.3	6.8	4.5	11.1	6.0	8.3	14.6	10.3	17.0
Internal sources:										
retentions	53.1	48.9	38.2	45.1	24.9	50.8	35.3	25.4	34.3	18.0
depreciation	41.9	41.3	33.1	38.0	24.4	44.3	51.6	35.8	43.8	21.7
Total sources:	99.9	99.8	99.9	100.0	99.9	99.9	100.0	99.8	99.7	99.8
Uses of funds (%)										
Fixed assets:										
tangible: 'replacement'	41.9	41.3	33.1	38.0	24.4	44.3	51.6	35.8	43.8	21.7
net	29.5	30.3	29.0	29.6	30.7	31.0	27.6	24.1	26.9	20.4
intangible	0.8	0.9	1.3	1.0	1.7	0.5	1.2	1.1	1.0	0.5
subsidiaries and trade investments	0	2.8	35.7	16.1	68.4	0	2.5	47.4	20.1	68.0
Stocks	21.0	26.5	29.3	26.8	25.1	27.2	27.2	26.3	26.8	21.0
Bank and cash balances	−1.1	−8.0	−15.1	−9.9	−17.1	1.5	−5.9	−13.4	−7.5	−14.0
Net trade credit given	10.8	10.4	9.2	10.0	4.7	7.7	1.6	−0.2	2.1	−2.2
Other current assets, provisions and sundry items	−2.9	−4.5	−22.7	−11.8	−38.1	−12.3	−5.9	−21.2	−13.4	−15.5
Total uses:	100.0	99.7	99.8	99.8	99.8	99.9	100.0	99.9	99.8	99.9

Notes:
Total sources ≡ Total users.   Fuller definitions of the variables are given in appendix B.   Accounts sometimes fail to sum to 100% because of rounding.

Table D.D   Appropriation of income: analysis by expenditure on acquisitions

	1948–64					1964–71				
	Zero	Low	High	All companies	Top 100	Zero	Low	High	All companies	Top 100
Income (%)										
depreciation	16.9	19.4	19.4	19.0	19.2	20.2	26.2	26.9	25.3	25.0
operating profit	80.0	77.4	77.1	77.7	77.9	76.1	69.7	69.2	70.8	71.4
dividends and interest received	2.1	2.6	2.8	2.6	2.4	3.0	3.5	3.4	3.4	3.2
other income	0.8	0.4	0.5	0.5	0.4	0.6	0.4	0.3	0.4	0.2
total:	99.8	99.8	99.8	99.8	99.9	99.9	99.8	99.8	99.9	99.8
Appropriations (%)										
depreciation	16.9	19.4	19.4	19.0	19.2	20.2	26.2	26.9	25.3	25.0
interest paid (gross)	1.4	1.5	2.2	1.8	2.6	2.1	4.2	5.7	4.4	6.9
taxation	42.6	40.2	39.7	40.4	39.2	41.2	36.9	37.2	37.9	37.8
dividends: ordinary (net)	16.8	15.3	15.9	15.8	17.6	15.4	14.6	14.4	14.7	13.6
pref. (net)	2.7	2.3	2.1	2.3	1.9	1.2	1.1	0.7	1.0	0.7
minority interests and prior-year adjustments	-0.1	0.3	0.5	0.3	0.9	-0.1	-0.1	-0.3	-0.2	0.1
retained profits	19.5	20.8	19.8	20.2	18.3	19.9	16.8	15.1	16.7	15.6
total:	99.8	99.8	99.6	99.8	99.7	99.9	99.7	99.7	99.8	99.7
Cost of dividends (% of total income):										
ordinary	19.7	17.9	18.3	18.4	19.6	25.0	23.6	23.4	23.8	22.4
preference	3.3	2.8	2.6	2.8	2.2	1.9	1.8	1.2	1.6	1.1

Notes:
Income ≡ Appropriations.   Fuller definitions of the variables are given in appendix B.   Accounts sometimes fail to sum to 100% because of rounding.

Table D.E Balance sheets (1948 and 1964): analysis by expenditure on acquisitions

	1948					1964				
	Zero	Low	High	All companies	Top 100	Zero	Low	High	All companies	Top 100
Assets (%)										
Fixed assets:										
tangible (net)	45.8	41.3	42.1	42.3	41.0	54.8	51.9	54.0	53.3	58.4
intangible	3.5	5.2	6.2	5.3	10.5	1.0	1.7	5.1	3.0	11.0
trade investments	0.2	2.9	2.7	2.4	2.3	0	0.1	0.5	0.3	0.9
total:	49.5	49.4	51.0	50.0	53.8	55.8	53.7	59.6	56.6	70.3
Current assets:										
stocks	40.5	43.1	42.3	42.3	37.1	34.2	40.0	41.3	39.6	39.6
net liquidity	20.6	19.5	18.1	19.1	24.0	8.7	4.1	-2.5	2.1	-7.0
other current assets	-10.7	-12.1	-11.6	-11.7	-15.0	1.1	2.0	1.5	1.6	-3.0
total:	99.9	99.9	99.8	99.7	99.9	99.8	99.8	99.9	99.9	99.9
Financing (%)										
Equity interest:										
ordinary shares	32.6	28.8	30.3	30.0	38.4	37.8	35.9	35.0	35.8	33.5
reserves	37.9	40.6	38.9	39.5	35.2	44.5	45.1	42.1	43.7	39.4
	70.5	69.4	69.2	69.5	73.6	82.3	81.0	77.1	79.5	72.9
Preference shares	18.0	17.2	16.9	17.2	14.7	8.5	7.8	6.8	7.5	5.8
Long-term loans	3.0	3.6	3.6	3.5	2.2	3.6	5.0	8.7	6.3	11.9
Future tax reserves	7.7	7.9	8.0	7.9	8.1	5.3	5.0	5.1	5.1	5.7
Minority interests	0.5	1.7	2.1	1.7	1.2	0.1	1.1	2.1	1.4	3.4
Total:	99.7	99.8	99.8	99.8	99.8	99.8	99.9	99.8	99.8	99.7

Notes:

Assets = Financing.

Fuller definitions of the variables are given in appendix B.

Accounts sometimes fail to sum to 100% because of rounding.

Table D.F   Balance sheets (1964 and 1971): analysis by expenditure on acquisitions

	1964					1971				
	Zero	Low	High	All companies	Top 100	Zero	Low	High	All companies	Top 100
Assets (%)										
Fixed assets:										
tangible (net)	57.2	54.6	52.8	54.4	48.6	60.3	59.7	60.3	60.1	58.5
intangible	1.8	3.4	5.0	3.8	7.0	1.2	2.5	7.8	4.4	13.4
trade investments	0	0.2	0.5	0.3	0.8	0	0.2	0.5	0.3	0.7
total:	59.0	58.2	58.3	58.5	56.4	61.5	62.4	68.6	64.8	72.6
Current assets:										
stocks	36.9	42.3	41.7	41.0	49.7	39.4	45.9	48.5	45.7	54.2
net liquidity	7.8	-0.3	-0.6	1.2	-6.3	6.5	-2.8	-9.3	-3.6	-16.4
other current assets	-3.8	-0.4	0.5	-0.7	0	-7.5	-5.7	-8.1	-7.0	-10.5
total:	99.9	99.8	99.9	100.0	99.8	99.9	99.8	99.7	99.9	99.9
Financing (%)										
Equity interest:										
ordinary shares	37.3	36.3	37.3	36.9	36.5	32.8	31.5	30.4	31.3	26.3
reserves	42.6	40.9	40.6	41.1	39.0	56.2	50.7	47.5	50.5	46.3
	79.9	77.2	77.9	78.0	75.5	89.0	82.2	77.9	81.8	72.6
Preference shares	8.0	6.5	5.3	6.3	4.9	4.8	4.3	2.8	3.8	2.7
Long-term loans	4.2	7.7	7.4	6.9	8.7	5.7	11.1	16.1	12.1	20.8
Future tax reserves	7.7	6.4	7.1	6.9	8.3	0.3	0.5	0.6	0.5	0.5
Minority interests	0.1	1.9	2.1	1.6	2.4	0.1	1.8	2.4	1.7	3.1
Total:	99.9	99.7	99.8	99.7	99.8	99.9	99.9	99.8	99.9	99.7

Notes:

Assets ≡ Financing.

Fuller definitions of the variables are given in appendix B.

Accounts sometimes fail to sum to 100% because of rounding.

Table D.G Growth, financing ratios, etc.: analysis by gross investment in fixed assets

Percentage per annum

	1948–64					1964–71				
	Low	Middle	High	All companies	Top 100	Low	Middle	High	All companies	Top 100
Growth:										
of net assets[a]	5.5	8.0	13.3	9.0	18.6	7.4	9.6	18.5	11.8	27.3
by gross fixed investment[a]	3.0	6.6	12.9	7.5	20.0	4.0	8.5	17.3	8.9	26.0
by net fixed investment[a]	0.9	3.1	7.0	3.7	11.3	0.6	3.6	9.1	4.4	14.5
by takeover[a]: total	1.1	1.6	3.5	2.1	5.6	3.0	3.6	8.0	4.9	13.5
for cash	n.a.	n.a.	n.a.	n.a.	n.a.	1.4	1.6	2.9	1.7	4.8
by issue	n.a.	n.a.	n.a.	n.a.	n.a.	1.7	2.1	5.1	3.2	8.8
book value	n.a.	n.a.	n.a.	n.a.	n.a.	2.1	2.8	5.4	3.4	8.8
by retention[a]	3.9	5.5	7.2	5.5	8.7	3.3	4.6	7.8	5.1	10.6
by external finance[a]: total	1.0	1.9	5.4	2.7	9.3	3.1	4.0	9.5	5.5	15.2
exchange	n.a.	n.a.	n.a.	n.a.	n.a.	2.1	2.3	5.2	3.2	8.9
Pre-tax rate of profit[b]	15.8	18.1	19.9	17.9	20.0	14.8	17.7	20.1	17.5	22.1
Opening size (£ million)	2.142	2.902	2.607	2.551	2.420	12.738	13.645	10.385	12.256	6.042
Number of companies	415	417	418	1250	101	322	322	322	966	100

Notes:
[a] Percent of opening net assets.
[b] Percent of average net assets.

See appendix B for fuller definitions.

101

Table D.H. Sources and uses of funds: analysis by gross investment in fixed assets

	1948–64					1964–71				
	Low	Middle	High	All com-panies	Top 100	Low	Middle	High	All com-panies	Top 100
Sources of funds (%)										
Issues of ordinary shares:										
for cash						2.9	2.9	6.0	4.0	8.2
in exchange						7.1	7.3	9.6	8.0	11.5
total:	7.5	10.3	17.2	11.7	20.6	10.0	10.2	15.6	12.0	19.7
Issues of preference shares:										
for cash						−1.9	−0.5	−0.2	−0.9	0
in exchange						0.3	0.2	0.2	0.2	0.2
total:	−0.4	1.1	1.2	0.7	1.6	−1.6	−0.3	0	−0.7	0.2
Issues of long-term loans:										
for cash						5.8	7.6	9.6	7.6	8.2
in exchange						3.6	2.2	2.4	2.7	3.1
total:	2.0	3.8	7.6	4.5	8.5	9.4	9.8	12.0	10.3	11.3
Internal sources:										
retentions	52.9	46.8	35.6	45.1	29.1	36.8	35.8	30.4	34.3	26.1
depreciation	37.9	37.8	38.3	38.0	40.1	45.2	44.5	41.7	43.8	42.5
Total sources:	99.9	99.8	99.9	100.0	99.9	99.8	100.0	99.7	99.7	99.8
Uses of funds (%)										
Fixed assets										
tangible 'replacement' net	37.9	37.8	38.3	38.0	40.1	45.2	44.5	41.7	43.8	42.5
net	13.9	33.4	41.4	29.6	45.0	6.7	31.9	42.0	26.9	48.3
intangible subsidiaries and trade	1.3	1.0	0.8	1.0	0.8	1.0	1.1	0.9	1.0	0.7
investments	17.1	14.7	16.7	16.1	16.7	19.5	18.6	22.2	20.1	26.3
Stocks	31.0	27.7	21.6	26.8	20.4	25.7	26.6	28.2	26.8	27.4
Bank and cash balances	−13.6	−9.2	−6.7	−9.9	−6.4	−1.6	−10.7	−10.0	−7.5	−11.9
Net trade credit given	18.3	7.3	4.5	10.0	−1.0	8.3	2.7	−4.8	2.1	−11.2
Other current assets, provisions and sundry items	−6.0	−12.7	−16.7	−11.8	−15.8	−4.9	−14.7	−20.4	−13.4	−22.2
Total uses:	99.9	100.0	99.9	99.8	99.8	99.9	100.0	99.8	99.8	99.9

Notes:
Total sources = Total uses.   Fuller definitions of the variables are given in appendix B.   Accounts sometimes fail to sum to 100% because of rounding.

Table D.I.   Appropriation of income: analysis by gross investment in fixed assets

	1948–64					1964–71				
	Low	Middle	High	All companies	Top 100	Low	Middle	High	All companies	Top 100
Income (%)										
Depreciation	14.1	18.4	24.4	19.0	30.3	22.1	23.6	30.2	25.3	37.2
Operating profit	81.4	78.4	73.4	77.7	67.8	72.3	72.6	67.4	70.8	60.3
Dividends and interest received	3.6	2.6	1.7	2.6	1.5	4.9	3.1	2.0	3.4	1.8
Other income	0.8	0.4	0.3	0.5	0.2	0.5	0.4	0.3	0.4	0.6
Total:	99.9	99.8	99.8	99.8	99.8	99.8	99.7	99.9	99.9	99.9
Appropriations (%)										
Depreciation	14.1	18.4	24.4	19.0	30.3	22.1	23.6	30.2	25.3	37.2
Interest paid (gross)	1.8	1.5	2.1	1.8	2.4	5.2	3.7	4.2	4.4	3.8
Taxation	44.4	41.0	35.9	40.4	31.0	40.7	39.0	34.0	37.9	30.3
Dividends: ordinary (net)	17.3	15.4	14.7	15.8	13.7	16.6	15.2	12.3	14.7	10.7
pref. (net)	3.3	2.2	1.4	2.3	1.1	1.3	1.0	0.6	1.0	0.4
Minority interests and prior year adjustments	0.4	0.3	0.3	0.3	0.3	-0.2	-0.3	0	-0.2	-0.2
Retained profits	18.5	20.9	21.0	20.2	20.9	14.0	17.4	18.6	16.7	17.5
Total:	99.8	99.7	99.8	99.8	99.7	99.7	99.6	99.9	99.8	99.7
Cost of dividends (% of total income):										
ordinary	20.4	17.9	16.8	18.4	15.3	26.7	24.6	20.0	23.8	17.5
preference	4.1	2.6	1.7	2.8	1.3	2.2	1.6	1.0	1.6	0.7

Notes:

Income ≡ Appropriations.

Fuller definitions of the variables are given in appendix B.

Accounts sometimes fail to sum to 100% because of rounding.

Table D.J Balance sheets (1948 and 1964): analysis by gross investment in fixed assets

	1948					1964				
	Low	Middle	High	All companies	Top 100	Low	Middle	High	All companies	Top 100
Assets (%)										
Fixed assets:										
tangible (net)	37.2	39.9	49.8	42.3	57.1	42.1	52.8	64.9	53.3	72.5
intangible	6.3	4.4	5.4	5.3	6.5	3.0	2.3	3.6	3.0	5.7
trade investments	2.7	2.1	2.4	2.4	2.2	0.2	0.4	0.2	0.3	0.4
	46.2	46.4	57.6	50.0	65.8	45.3	55.5	68.7	56.6	78.6
Current assets:										
stocks	44.4	43.8	38.8	42.3	38.7	43.6	40.9	34.4	39.6	34.7
net liquidity	19.3	20.8	17.2	19.1	17.7	3.9	2.8	−0.4	2.1	−3.2
other current assets	−10.1	−11.1	−13.8	−11.7	−22.4	7.0	0.7	−2.8	1.6	−10.1
total:	99.8	99.9	99.8	99.7	99.8	99.8	99.9	99.9	99.9	100.0
Financing (%)										
Equity interests:										
ordinary shares	29.4	28.3	32.4	30.0	34.0	35.2	36.2	35.9	35.8	33.8
reserves	38.0	41.9	38.5	39.5	38.6	44.7	44.3	42.1	43.7	43.0
	67.4	70.2	70.9	69.5	72.6	79.9	80.5	78.0	79.5	76.8
Preference shares	18.9	16.4	16.3	17.2	12.9	9.6	7.4	5.5	7.5	4.3
Long-term loans	4.2	3.3	3.1	3.5	4.2	4.1	5.2	9.6	6.3	12.1
Future tax reserves	7.4	8.3	8.1	7.9	8.1	4.8	5.2	5.3	5.1	4.9
Minority interests	1.8	1.6	1.5	1.7	2.0	1.3	1.3	1.5	1.4	1.7
Total:	99.7	99.8	99.9	99.8	99.8	99.7	99.6	99.9	99.8	99.9

Notes:

Assets = Financing.

Fuller definitions of the variables are given in appendix B.

Accounts sometimes fail to sum to 100% because of rounding.

Table D.K Balance sheets (1964 and 1971): analysis by gross investment in fixed assets

	1964					1971				
	Low	Middle	High	All companies	Top 100	Low	Middle	High	All companies	Top 100
Assets (%)										
Fixed assets:										
tangible (net)	49.1	52.1	61.9	54.4	68.0	49.7	58.0	72.6	60.1	85.8
intangible	3.6	2.8	4.9	3.8	6.1	4.0	4.0	5.2	4.4	6.3
trade investments	0.5	0.2	0.2	0.3	0.1	0.4	0.2	0.3	0.3	0.5
	53.2	55.1	67.0	58.5	74.2	54.1	62.2	78.1	64.8	92.6
Current assets:										
stocks	41.0	39.3	42.6	41.0	47.5	45.0	44.1	48.0	45.7	52.8
net liquidity	1.8	4.7	-3.1	1.2	-8.0	0.4	-2.4	-8.8	-3.6	-14.9
other current assets	3.9	0.7	-6.7	-0.7	-13.8	0.4	-4.0	-17.4	-7.0	-30.8
total:	99.9	99.8	99.8	100.0	99.9	99.9	99.9	99.9	99.9	99.7
Financing (%)										
Equity interests:										
ordinary shares	35.4	37.5	37.7	36.9	37.2	32.4	32.0	29.5	31.3	28.6
reserves	41.9	41.1	40.3	41.1	39.2	49.7	50.7	51.0	50.5	52.1
	77.3	78.6	78.0	78.0	76.4	82.1	82.7	80.5	81.8	80.7
Preference shares	7.0	6.4	5.5	6.3	5.0	4.5	3.9	2.9	3.8	2.2
Long-term loans	7.7	6.1	7.0	6.9	8.1	11.4	11.1	13.8	12.1	13.9
Future tax reserves	6.0	7.2	7.7	6.9	8.5	0.4	0.5	0.6	0.5	0.9
Minority interests	1.7	1.5	1.7	1.6	1.7	1.4	1.6	2.1	1.7	2.1
Total:	99.7	99.8	99.9	99.7	99.7	99.8	99.8	99.9	99.9	99.8

Notes:

Assets = Financing.

Fuller definitions of the variables are given in Appendix B.

Accounts sometimes fail to sum to 100% because of rounding.

Table D.L   The relation of the population of acquirers studied in the single merger study of chapter 3 with the population of companies which continued from 1964–71

	Acquirers studied in single merger study		All continuing companies (1964–71)	
	No.	% of continuing acquirers	No.	% of continuing acquirers
Top half by rate of growth by acquisition (A) of continuing companies with non-zero values of A	131	78.9	390	50.1
Bottom half by A of continuing companies with non-zero values of A	32	19.3	388	49.9
Companies with zero values of A	3[a]	1.8	188	
Companies not continuing from 1964 to 1971	45		0	
Companies excluded from the study of all continuing companies because of extreme values for some variable(s)	2		0	
Total:	213	100.0	966	100.0
Top 100 by A of continuing companies with non-zero values of A	38	22.9	100	12.9

[a]Their takeover occured in 1972 after the close of the period studied for all continuing companies.

Table D.M   The percentage of companies in the top third of the ranking by rate of growth by gross new investment belonging to the high, middle and low thirds of the ranking by profitability

Third by profitability	1948–64	1964–71
High	42.8	44.1
Middle	34.4	35.4
Low	22.7	20.5

Note:
See appendix B for fuller definitions.

References

Aaronovitch, S. and Sawyer, M.C. (1975). *Big Business*. London: Macmillan.

Accounting Standards Steering Committee (1973). Proposed Statement of Standard Accounting Practice: *Accounting for Changes in the Purchasing Power of Money*. Institute of Chartered Accountants in England and Wales, January 1973.

Accounting Standards Steering Committee (1974). Provisional Statement of Standard Accounting Practice, Number 7: *Accounting for Changes in the Purchasing Power of Money*. Institute of Chartered Accountants in England and Wales, June 1974.

Baumol, W.J. (1965). *The Stock Market and Economic Efficiency*. New York: Fordham University Press.

Berle, A.A. and Means, G. (1932). *The Modern Corporation and Private Property*. New York.

Bird, P. (1971). *The Interpretation of Published Accounts*. London: H.M.S.O.

Central Statistical Office (1963). *Economic Trends,* April 1963.

Central Statistical Office (1972). *National Income and Expenditure*. London: H.M.S.O.

Chartered Accountants' Trust for Education and Research (1967). *Accounting Requirements of the Companies Acts 1948–1967.* London: Gee and Co.

Chartered Accountants' Trust for Education and Research (1972). *Survey of Published Accounts, 1970–71.*

Cosh, A. (1975). 'The Remuneration of Chief Executives in the United Kingdom', *Economic Journal,* March 1975.

Cyert, R.M. and March, J.G. (1963). *A Behavioural Theory of the Firm*. Englewood Cliffs, N.J.: Prentice Hall.

Davis, E. and Yeomans, K. (1975). *Company Finance and the Capital Market, A Study of the Effects of Firm Size*. London: Cambridge University Press.

Department of Accounting and Business Method (1974). *Computer File of U.K. Quoted Companies' Accounts: 1948–71:* Notes on the Data. University of Edinburgh (duplicated booklet).

Department of Employment (1976). *Gazette,* 26 February 1976.

Department of Industry (1969–75). *Business Monitor, M.3:* Company Finance.

Department of Industry (1975). *Business Monitor, M7:* Acquisitions and Mergers of Companies: Fourth quarter, 1974: February 1975.

Department of Trade and Industry (1970). *Survey of Mergers*. London: H.M.S.O.

Galbraith, J.K. (1972). *The New Industrial State*. London: Andre Deutsch. Revised edition.

George, K.D. (1971). *Industrial Organisation*. London: George Allen and Unwin. First Edition.

George, K.D. (1972). 'The Large Firm in Modern Society', *Journal of Industrial Economics,* April 1972.

George, K.D. and Silberston, A. (1975). 'The Causes and Effects of Mergers', *Scottish Journal of Political Economy,* June 1975.

Gribbin, J.D. (1974). 'The Operation of the Mergers Panel since 1965', *Trade and Industry,* 17 January 1974.

Hart, P.E., Utton, M.A. and Walshe, G. (1973). *Mergers and Concentration in British Industry*. London: Cambridge University Press.

Hicks, J.R. (1935). 'The Theory of Monopoly', *Econometrica,* 1935.

Hindley, B. (1973). 'Take-overs: "Victims" and "Victors" ', in *Institute of Economic Affairs, Readings 10.* London: I.E.A.

Hogarty, T.F. (1970). 'The Profitability of Corporate Mergers', *Journal of Business,* 1970.

Howe, G. (1973). 'Government Policy on Mergers', *Trade and Industry,* November 1973.

Jones, C.J., Tweedie, D.P. and Whittington, G. (1976). 'The Regression Portfolio', *Journal of Business Finance and Accounting,* 1976.

Kalecki, M. (1937). 'The Principle of Increasing Risk', *Economica,* 1937.

Kelly, E.M. (1967). *The Profitability of Growth Through Mergers.* Pennsylvania State University.

Keynes, J.M. (1936). *The General Theory of Employment, Interest and Money.* London: Macmillan.

Kitching, J. (1967). 'Why do Mergers Miscarry?' *Harvard Business Review,* 1967.

Kuehn, D.A. (1975). *Takeovers and the Theory of the Firm.* London: Macmillan.

Lee, T.A. (1974). 'Accounting for and Disclosure of Business Combinations', *Journal of Business Finance and Accounting,* Spring 1974.

Leibenstein, H. (1966). 'Allocative Efficiency vs. "X-Efficiency" ', *American Economic Review,* 1966.

Lev, B. and Mandelker, G. (1972) 'The Microeconomic Consequences of Corporate Mergers', *Journal of Business,* 1972.

Lorie, J.H. and Halpern, P. (1970). 'Conglomerates: The Rhetoric and the Evidence', *Journal of Law and Economics,* 1970.

Marris, R. (1963). *The Economic Theory of 'Managerial' Capitalism.* London: Macmillan.

Marris, R. (1964). 'Incomes Policies−The Rate of Profit in Industry', *Transactions of the Manchester Statistical Society,* December 1964.

McClelland, W.G. (1972). 'The IRC 1966/71: An Experimental Prod', *Three Banks Review,* June 1972.

Meeks, G. (1974). 'Profit Illusion', *Bulletin of Oxford University Institute of Economics and Statistics,* November 1974.

Meeks, G. and Whittington, G. (1975a). 'Directors' Pay, Growth and Profitability', *Journal of Industrial Economics,* September 1975.

Meeks, G. and Whittington, G. (1975b). 'Giant Companies in the United Kingdom, 1948−69', *Economic Journal,* December 1975.

Meeks, G. and Whittington, G. (1976). *The Financing of Quoted Companies in the United Kingdom,* Background Paper No. 1, Royal Commission on the Distribution of Income and Wealth. London: H.M.S.O.

National Institute of Economic and Social Research (1956). *Company Income and Finance, 1949−53.* London: National Institute of Economic and Social Research.

Neild, R.R. (1963). *Pricing and Employment in the Trade Cycle.* London: Cambridge University Press.

Newbould, G.D. (1970). *Management and Merger Activity.* Liverpool: Guthstead.

Parker, R.H. (1972). *Understanding Company Financial Statements.* Harmondsworth: Penguin.

Penrose, E.T. (1959). *The Theory of the Growth of the Firm.* Oxford: Basil Blackwell.

Pratten, C. (1971). *Economies of Scale in Manufacturing Industry.* London: Cambridge University Press.

Pratten, C. and Dean, R.M. with Silberston, A. (1965). *The Economies of Large Scale Production in British Industry.* London: Cambridge University Press.

Reddaway, W.B. (1967). 'Higgledy Piggledy Growth', *Economic Journal,* 1967.

Reddaway, W.B. (1970). *Effects of the Selective Employment Tax.* London: H.M.S.O.

Reid, S.R. (1968). *Mergers, Managers and the Economy.* New York.

Revans, R.S. (1960). 'Morale and the Size of the Working Group', in Schilling, R.S.F., ed., *Modern Trends in Occupational Health.* London: Butterworth.

Richardson, G.B. (1972). 'The Organisation of Industry', *Economic Journal,* 1972.

Robbins, Lord (1973). 'Summing Up: Mergers and the Legal Framework', in *Institute of Economic Affairs, Readings 10.* London: I.E.A.

Robinson, J. (1964). *Economic Philosophy.* Harmondsworth: Penguin

Rose, H.B. and Newbould, G.D. (1967). 'The 1967 take-over boom', *Moorgate and Wall Street,* 1967.

Rowley, C.K. and Peacock, A.T. (1975). *Welfare Economics. A Liberal Restatement.* London: M. Robertson.

Rowthorn, R. (1971). *International Big Business, 1957–67.* London: Cambridge University Press.

Ryden, B. *Mergers in Swedish Industry.* Stockholm: Amquist and Wicksell.

Samuels, J.M. and Smyth, D.J. (1968). 'Profits, Variability of Profits and Firm Size', *Economica,* 1968.

Sandilands Committee (1975). *Inflation Accounting.* Cmnd 6225. London: H.M.S.O.

Servan-Schreiber, J.J. (1968). *The American Challenge.* London: H. Hamilton.

Shonfield, A. (1965). *Modern Capitalism.* London: Oxford University Press.

Singh, A. (1971). *Takeovers.* London: Cambridge University Press.

Singh, A. (1975). 'Takeovers, Economic Natural Selection, and the Theory of the Firm: Evidence from the Postwar United Kingdom Experience', *Economic Journal,* September 1975.

Singh, A. (1976). Review of Kuehn (1975), *Journal of Economic Literature,* July 1976.

Singh, A. and Whittington, G. (1968). *Growth, Profitability and Valuation.* London: Cambridge University Press.

Smyth, D.J., Boyes, W.J. and Peseau, D.E. (1975). *Size, Growth, Profits and Executive Compensation in the Large Corporation.* London: Macmillan.

Sutherland, A. (1969). *The Monopolies Commission in Action.* London: Cambridge University Press.

Sutherland, A. (1971). 'The Management of Mergers Policy', in Cairncross, A. (ed.), *The Managed Economy.* Oxford: Basil Blackwell.

Sutherland, A. (1975). Comment on 'British Merger Policy', in George, K.D. and Joll, D., eds., *Competition Policy in the U.K. and E.E.C.* London: Cambridge University Press.

Taylor, Lord, of Harlow (1976). Letter to *The Times,* headed 'Advantages of Small Firms', 3 March 1976.

Times (1976). 'Financial Editorial', *The Times,* 21 June 1976.

Utton, M.A. (1971). 'The Effects of Mergers on Concentration: U.K. Manufacturing Industry, 1954–65', *Journal of Industrial Economics,* November 1971.

Utton, M.A. (1974). 'On Measuring the Effects of Industrial Mergers', *Scottish Journal of Political Economy,* 1974.

Utton, M.A. (1975). 'British Merger Policy', in George, K.D. and Joll, C., eds., *Competition Policy in the U.K. and E.E.C.* London: Cambridge University Press.

Weaver, G. (1971). *Investment Analysis.* London: Longman.

Whittington, G. (1971). *The Prediction of Profitability, and Other Studies of Company Behaviour.* London: Cambridge University Press.

Whittington, G. (1972). 'Changes in the Top 100 Quoted Manufacturing Companies in the United Kingdom, 1948 to 1968', *Journal of Industrial Economics,* November 1972.

Whittington, G. (1972). 'The Profitability of Retained Earnings', *Review of Economics and Statistics,* 1972.

Whittington, G. (1974). *Company Taxation and Dividends.* Institute for Fiscal Studies, Lecture Series Number 1.

Wigham, E. (1976). 'Small is Peaceful', *The Times,* 26 February 1976.

Wood, A. (1975). *A Theory of Profits.* London: Cambridge University Press.